TIME IS MONEY

The Power Of Non-Directional Options Trading

D0988993

Kerry W. Given, Ph.D.
Founder, Parkwood Capital, LLC
Co-Founder, G&L Capital Management, LLC

Time is Money
Copyright ©2015 Kerry W. Given

ISBN 978-1622-877-57-7 HC
ISBN 978-1622-877-58-4 PRINT
ISBN 978-1622-877-60-7 EBOOK

LCCN 2014955899

February 2015

Published and Distributed by
First Edition Design Publishing, Inc.
P.O. Box 20217, Sarasota, FL 34276-3217
www.firsteditiondesignpublishing.com

*To Charlotte, my best friend, confidante and adviser.
I am a better person due to your influence in my life.*

*In memory of our son and fellow option trader,
Sean (1975 - 2007). I miss our discussions of Google.*

Acknowledgments

When I look back over my life to this point, I realize that I owe this book and many other accomplishments to my wife, Charlotte, who has been a wonderful life partner. I am a better person because of her being in my life. Her unwavering support, influence, and excellent advice have been crucial to my success.

I owe thanks to many teachers, especially Jim Bittman and Russell Rhoads at the Options Institute of the Chicago Board Options Exchange. My continued conversations with Jim Bittman through the years have been enlightening. His support and advice have been invaluable for both my options trading and the development of this book.

Most of all, I wish to thank my students. Their support and encouragement are very much appreciated. Through the years, I have listened to my students and learned of the common misunderstandings and pitfalls that face beginning options traders. My coaching courses and this book are better products as a result.

Ray Lilja was my first coaching student in 2007 and that led to the start-up of Parkwood Capital, LLC. His support and encouragement have led to our partnership in founding G&L Capital Management, LLC. Thank you, Ray, for your trust and support.

Royal Ellinger, D.D.S., graciously offered to read the first draft of the manuscript and his comments and observations have resulted in this being a much better book. Thank you, Royal, for the time and thought you invested in this project.

Table of Contents

Introduction

Traders love to make predictions. Even better, they enjoy collecting a nice profit when their prediction proves to be correct. This may be the most fundamental sense of satisfaction that traders enjoy. Many successful traders have been interviewed through the years and a common assertion is that making money wasn't the source of their motivation; they often regard the money as only a "score card" of sorts. The core sense of accomplishment arose from the thrill of the hunt and the satisfaction of having one's analysis being proven correct.

For some traders, the analysis of the fundamentals of a company and/or a market is the principal activity leading to their conclusion to buy a particular stock or an options position on that stock. This may include a detailed analysis of the balance sheet and various financial figures, such as book value, debt to equity ratios, current assets to current liabilities ratios, and many more financial measures. Many fundamental analysts track the price to earning ratio and analyze the business prospects to attempt to predict the future earnings stream. The most famous of the fundamental analysts, Warren Buffett, emphasizes the comparison of the company's book value to the current stock price. Buffett's mentor, Benjamin Graham, outlined the best case for fundamental analysis of stocks in his famous book, *The Intelligent Investor*.

Other traders rely on technical analysis, focusing exclusively on the stock's price chart. John Murphy is one of the best-known technical analysts, and his book, *Technical Analysis of the Financial Markets*, remains a best seller. The essence of technical analysis is that all of the relevant information for the trader is contained in the stock's price and volume behavior. Technical analysts draw trend lines, identify levels of support and resistance, analyze candlestick patterns, monitor trading volume, plot the Bollinger bands, calculate various statistical measures, and so on.

Many traders employ a combination of both fundamental and technical analysis. Regardless of the techniques used for the analysis, a significant amount of work and study goes into the trader's thought process that leads to the initiation of the trade.

Therefore, the trader has invested a lot of time and thought into the trade even before she invests her hard earned capital. It is easy to figuratively walk away from an activity or hobby where I have not invested any time. But as I devote more time and analysis to the project, my level of personal ownership grows. In many avenues of life that principle serves us well. Industrial empires have been built largely due to the perseverance of the entrepreneur who was determined that his product or service was indeed superior. But this same principle can be the undoing of the trader. Many traders continue to invest in a position and buy additional shares of a stock as the price declines, all the while telling everyone how his analysis concludes that the stock is trading at a bargain price. I remember friends telling me how they were buying Lucent and WorldCom at bargain basement prices and urged me to get on board. To their surprise, those stocks continued to trade lower and lower. Similar behavior occurs when the trader holds a losing position and the losses continue to build; he is convinced that his analysis will be proven correct and the investment will turn around "soon". His pride is on the line.

It is extremely difficult for the trader to admit that his analysis was wrong and close the trade. Losing the money is actually easier than admitting that all of that research and deductive reasoning was somehow flawed. And this is magnified if he told several of his friends about this stock and urged them to take advantage of this trade. How does he tell them he was wrong?

Many, if not all of us traders, have capital to trade because we have been successful in some other career. A successful attorney doesn't succeed when he misses critical case law 30% of the time. Imagine going to a surgeon to have your appendix removed and the nurse tells you this surgeon is pretty good; he only loses patients in appendectomies a few times every month. The typical professional who is learning to trade stocks and/or options has spent twenty or thirty years in his career environment of high percentage play. He has been trained that hard work and extra effort will make the difference between mediocre results and success.

It is certainly true that hard work and diligence in learning about the markets that one trades form a necessary foundation for success. But as the mathematicians say, hard work is a necessary, but not sufficient, condition for success in trading the markets.

The huge difference in trading from any of our previous careers is the win/loss ratio. Traders may make excellent profits over time with win/loss ratios of sixty or seventy percent. We intuitively find that fact hard to accept. In fact, we may even quietly think that we will do much better than that – after all, I have a Ph.D. or an M.D., or an engineering degree. I wasn't successful in my career by losing 30% of my cases, losing 30% of my patients, or only having one or two of the bridges I designed collapse. But many successful traders book 30% of their trades as losses and still show a profit at the end of the year.

Many successful professionals are perfectionists. That perfectionism has served them well in their professions. But it will be the death of a trader. This fundamental paradigm shift may well be the most difficult transition for the successful professional beginning the process of learning to trade. Successful people in many different walks of life share this tendency to perfectionism. Psychologists have frequently written of their very successful patients carrying deep-seated fears that they had not done enough or thinking to themselves that they could have done a better job. This is what drives them to succeed. When that person learns to trade, she will study the stock in great detail, analyze the price chart and learn everything possible about the company's business. Then she will enter the trade, convinced that her analysis is correct. Now fast forward a few days or weeks and we see that the stock has surprised everyone and is moving down in price. This new trader will revisit her analysis, and, convinced of her conclusions, will either stay in this position, or may even add additional capital to the position – because she is convinced her analysis is correct!

The process of analysis and action that has succeeded so many times in the past fails her in the markets. In fact, a common pattern is for this new trader to take that loss, but to work even harder on the analysis of the next potential investment. Accepting the fact that trading involves the occurrence of losing trades with reasonable frequency just never seems plausible. That principle is not even remotely consistent with anything she has learned about how to succeed in life. Trading is difficult not only because of the difficulty of predicting the future, but also because we must accept the fact that we will always have a rather large number of misses.

Predicting future price moves is difficult at best. Imagine not having to make any prediction whatsoever! That is the essence of non-directional trading. I don't try to predict where the market is going or when it will get there. I simply develop a system of rules that I use to react to whatever price moves the market may make each day. I don't predict the market's next move – I respond to the market's current move. These trading strategies benefit from the time decay of options. Time decay is a unique characteristic of options pricing that non-directional traders may use to their advantage.

But many of the psychological problems addressed above torture the non-directional trader as well. We will find ourselves in situations where our system's rules tell us to close or re-position an options spread. But we look at the price chart and identify a support level and think that maybe we should wait until that support level is broken before closing. Now we have added a directional prediction into our non-directional trading system – we have poisoned our system!

I have watched students make a similar error in hedging their non-directional trading positions. Often we use a long option to hedge our trade when the market moves against us. If the market then pulls back, we remove the hedge and have salvaged the original position. However, insurance is never free; we lose money on that hedge option. But we only lose a few percent of the maximum gains for the trade. On more than one occasion, I have observed students predict that the move up or down is over and the index is going to pull back. Then they remove the hedge early, <u>based on their prediction</u>. Of course, it is almost as though the market knows this and resumes its move higher or lower, driving the trader's position into a larger loss, because the hedge is now gone. A common error in non-directional trading is falling into the prediction trap. A secondary error is trying to save the cost of the insurance and taking a larger loss as a result.

One of the more important things I have learned in my non-directional trading is to follow my rules with great discipline and focus on the downside risk. If I manage the risk and ignore my "insurance cost", the gains take care of themselves.

The solution for many of these issues boils down to emotional control and maintaining the discipline to follow one's trading system. And this will continue to be a struggle for the non-directional trader. But try to imagine for a moment the freedom of not having to predict the market's direction. Imagine the diminished stress of no longer waking up with the first thought being the fear that the S&P 500 Index will gap up this morning in spite of a well reasoned case for the S&P 500 Index to trade downward. As one develops and refines her non-directional trading system, she will gain confidence in her system, her discipline will grow, and her stress will diminish.

In trading, as in all of life, there is no free lunch. I am certainly not suggesting that trading non-directionally is the "holy grail" or the "secret". But it is an attractive trading strategy and I think it is worth your time to learn more about how to "throw away your crystal ball" and trade non-directionally. That is the objective of this book.

CHAPTER ONE

WHAT IS NON-DIRECTIONAL TRADING?

Delta neutral trading is one of the buzzword phrases that has been used in marketing options trading education, trading alert services, and describing the strategies of hedge funds. Often, the sales people selling those services cannot articulate a succinct definition of the term or even tell you why it presents any advantages. They are just selling the buzzword. Delta neutral does sound exotic – is this the trading secret I have been searching for? Is this the secret strategy those evil market makers have been hiding from the little guy? But we will see clearly in this book that there is no "secret" to options trading. Many people will tell you they have the secret strategy used by the professionals on the floor of the exchange. When you hear or read that pitch, turn and go the other way. It's just marketing hype. Non-directional trading is a lesser known term and may be considered a subset of delta neutral trading. But at the end of this chapter, you will be able to define the delta neutral trade, describe the different opportunities where the trade might be used, and specify the advantages and disadvantages of delta neutral trading. Perhaps more importantly, we will distinguish delta neutral trading from non-directional trading. These are not synonyms.

Where Is My Risk?

Whenever we establish an options trade of any kind, we are exposed to risk from a change in one or more of three variables. The obvious factor affecting the profitability of our position is the price of the underlying stock or index. Most options traders began as stock traders and were trained to focus on the stock price. Whether I was short or long the stock, the price change represented my risk. When those stock traders begin to

̓1ey are often surprised by two additional factors that may
r diminish the profitability of their trade.

̲ɾatility is the second risk factor for our trade and this is a
̲ɾɯw concept for stock traders. We will discuss implied volatility in depth
in Chapter 5. For now, think of implied volatility as the market's
collective opinion of the future volatility of this stock or index price. Thus,
implied volatility may be higher than it has been historically for this stock
or index, or it may be lower. But in either case, it is essentially a prediction
of the range of future price movement; it is definitely not a prediction of
price direction. Beginning options traders often are surprised when their
prediction of price has proven correct, but their option value is unchanged
or only modestly profitable. The culprit is often implied volatility; during
the life of the trade, implied volatility has shifted up or down and this has
affected the value of the option position.

The third factor affecting the profitability of our position is time, or
more precisely, the passage of time. An experienced stock trader may be
surprised by the critical role of time in options trading. Stock traders often
rely on time as their safety valve. I may analyze ACME Manufacturing
and predict that the Wily Coyote is driving sales higher. My analysis
concludes that it will trade from its current price of $125 per share to
$150 over the next thirty days. So I buy ACME stock and check the price
every few days. Thirty days go by, and ACME is actually trading down
about $5. I revisit my analysis of ACME and decide my prediction is
correct, but the move will occur over a longer period of time. Time is my
friend – I can afford to wait for the stock price to go up as I predicted. Of
course, this ignores the opportunity cost of the investment, but most stock
traders are willing to give the position time to prove the original thesis
correct.

Trading options is fundamentally different from trading stock in one
key aspect: options are a decaying asset. I can afford to hold my stock
longer while waiting for the price to move upward. But that may not be
true of my options trade. Options positions always have some degree of
time sensitivity; in some cases, the option position is losing value as time
passes. Time is working against us. But other option positions display the
opposite time dependence; as long as the stock or index price doesn't

move too far, our position actually gains in value with the passage of time. For those positions, time is our friend.

So we are always exposed to risk in our options trading principally from three areas:

> Changes in the underlying stock or index price
> Changes in the implied volatility of the underlying stock or index
> The passage of time

Mathematical parameters have been developed to help us quantify the degree of risk in our options position due to changes in these variables. We call these mathematical parameters, the options Greeks. They received this name because Greek letters are used to symbolize each parameter (technically, one of the Greeks is not represented by a Greek letter, but that is another story).

Delta is the Greek that describes how much the profitability of my options position will increase or decrease with a change in the price of the underlying stock or index. When a trade has minimal dependence on the price movement of the underlying stock or index, we refer to this position as "delta neutral", i.e., the position is essentially neutral or indifferent to changes in the stock or index price. Some may refer to these strategies as "sideways" trades that may be deployed when the prediction for the underlying is for minimal price movement, or a "sideways" price move. We will discuss the Greeks in more detail in Chapter 4.

The Opportunistic Model

We may use a delta neutral trade in two very different ways, and it is important to know which strategy or trading philosophy we are using. Traders often have a small group of stocks they have followed for a long time; they understand their trading patterns, likely movements around earnings announcements, the normal ranges of volatility and so on. When the trader predicts a sideways trading range for the near future of one of the stocks she is following, a delta neutral options trade may be an excellent choice to benefit from that prediction, assuming the trader's prediction proves to be correct.

Other market factors, such as the current levels of implied volatility for this stock's options, may dictate the final selection of an appropriate delta neutral trading strategy for this stock.

In this case, the trader is using a delta neutral strategy because she is predicting a sideways price pattern or price movement within a modest sized channel. The delta neutral trade is just one choice among several strategies. If the trader is bullish, she selects a bullish trade; if she is bearish, she selects a bearish trade. And if her prediction is for essentially a sideways price movement, she selects a delta neutral trade.

The opportunistic delta neutral trading strategy is a directional trade; it is based on the trader's prediction for the future price movement of the underlying stock or market index. The directional trader has a specific interest with particular knowledge about an individual stock or index and a prediction for its future value.

The Insurance Model

The insurance model uses a delta neutral trade in a very different way. In this case, the trader has no prediction about the future value of the underlying stock or index. This trader positions the trade in such a way as to achieve a high probability of success and manages the position with a collection of rules that I refer to as a trading system. The trading system encompasses the trader's response to several critical questions:

➢ Under what circumstances do I enter the trade?
➢ How do I adjust the position if the underlying stock or index price moves against me?
➢ What adjustment technique will I use?
➢ What price or other measure will trigger my adjustment?
➢ Under what circumstances will I remove or close my adjustment?
➢ Where is my stop loss? Will it trigger automatically? If so, at what price?
➢ Is there a time stop for this position, i.e., a point in time where the trade will be closed irrespective of other variables?
➢ Is there a profit stop for this position, i.e., a level of profit that triggers a close of the position?

A trader should always have a trading system for any and all trades in his portfolio. When I am using delta neutral trades with the insurance model, two critical keys exist for my success:

1. a detailed, specific trading system that is written in my trading journal, and
2. strong personal discipline to follow the trading system rules promptly and unemotionally.

I refer to this trading strategy as the insurance model because of the similarities to running an insurance business. For example, consider the parallels in Table 1.1.

Table 1.1
The Insurance Model

Insurance Model Trading	Insurance Business
I have clearly defined the risk and developed a system to manage that risk.	Underwriters determine risk before any policies are written or priced.
The level of credits received by the options strategy is appropriate to generate a profit over the long term.	The premiums collected on the policies allow for payouts for the expected level of losses.
I follow the trading system rules with great discipline.	No special pricing of policies is offered for the agent's friends.
I employ my delta neutral trading strategy every month without predicting whether the next month will be a "good" month for this trade.	The agent sells policies all year without regard to weather or accident patterns; those patterns are priced into the premiums.
I am not predicting future market moves.	The insurance agent does not attempt to predict whether this will be a "good" year in his business.
I have a probabilistic edge in my trading system.	The underwriters have built a profit margin into the policy premium based on the risk profile.

One difference between the opportunistic and insurance models for trading delta neutral is the underlying stock or index. My prediction for a sideways price move could be applied to a particular stock at a particular point in time, but it could also be applied to a broad market index based on a sideways price prediction for the entire market.

The insurance model of non-directional options trading typically uses a broad market index for the delta neutral trade. This avoids the sudden price moves that are always possible for an individual stock due to stock-specific factors, e.g., an analyst downgrade, market reaction to the company's earnings announcement, the CFO is arrested for fraud, global events occur that primarily affect a particular industry sector, etc.

Non-Directional Trading

Most option traders come from a stock trading background. So we are accustomed to making a prediction for the stock price to rise or fall over some period of time. Options may be traded the same way, based on one's prediction for the underlying stock or index. I call this directional trading. It is based on a prediction of a price change over a particular period of time.

But options strategies offer stock traders a new alternative; the options trader can earn a profit on a stock that is just trading sideways. Options traders refer to these as delta neutral or sideways trades. But these strategies may be used in two rather different ways. I may study the underlying stock or even the overall market and predict a sideways pattern of prices for the next 30 days. I could then enter a delta neutral position, such as an iron condor, and profit if my prediction proves correct. This is the opportunistic model discussed above. This is directional trading; I have just predicted a sideways price direction.

I used the insurance model discussion above to illustrate the difference when we trade non-directionally. I distinguish non-directional trading from delta neutral trading in one critically important way. If I am trading non-directionally, I develop a series of rules for entry, exit and adjustment of a delta neutral trading strategy and then enter and manage the position dictated by those rules month after month. I have made no prediction of the future; I just manage the position each day based on the market's price move that day. I am no longer predicting the market's next move; I am reacting to what the market gives me today.

This may appear at first glance to be an argument that is splitting hairs, but the distinction is powerful. When I am relieved of the pressure of predicting tomorrow's price move, that relieves much of the stress of trading. When the market makes a move against my position, I just follow my rules to adjust the position. I don't refer to any technical indicators to predict future price moves and try to decide if an adjustment is needed. I follow my rules. This is the philosophy of non-directional trading and I find this to be a very powerful technique for relieving trading stress.

How should we use the option Greeks for the position? Some may suggest that following the position's Greeks is tantamount to following a technical indicator, such as the MACD. But the Greeks of the position assist the trader in monitoring the risk of the position and how that risk may have changed. Option Greeks are not predicting the future. The Greeks alert us to increased risk in a particular area, such as volatility or price movement, and this may trigger an adjustment of the position to moderate that risk. This is risk management, not a prediction of the future price movement of the underlying stock or index.

However, it is easy for the non-directional trader to "fall off the wagon". Whenever the market makes a move against your position, and you think that it will certainly pull back because your favorite technical indicator is screaming overbought, you are in danger of abandoning your system of non-directional trading rules. When expiration is approaching and you reason that this spread is safe and the index never moves that far overnight, you are in danger of abandoning your system of non-directional trading rules.

This is analogous to the insurance business discussed above. Insurance underwriters determine the risk of various events occurring for people in different categories of risk. The policy is priced based on that risk, so that sufficient funds will be available to pay claims, and yet also generate a profit. The insurance agent doesn't have the freedom to alter those rules. He doesn't charge more for the auto insurance policy purchased in September in Chicago because snow and fender-benders are coming. He knows that the underwriters have priced that risk into the policy. He follows the rules.

The non-directional trader uses delta neutral strategies in a similar way. He diligently avoids making any predictions about future price trends. This trader is deploying a delta neutral option trading strategy month after month with an underlying broad market index, using a system of trading and adjustment rules. The non-directional trader reacts to the market's price movements today, rather than predicting any future price movement. Each morning, as the market opens, he has a game plan dictated by the rules of his trading system. For example, his rules for the day might be:

> ➤ If the SPX index drops to $1810, I will adjust my position by buying three puts at the $1810 strike in the next month.
> ➤ If SPX trades up to $1895, I will adjust my position by buying three calls at the $1895 strike in the next month.
> ➤ If SPX stays in between these prices, I will take no action.

The specific actions above are not important; the point of this example is that each day presents the non-directional trader with a new unpredictable market and he has a specific set of actions that he will take based on the price movement of the stock or index being trading. *The non-directional trader is trading what he sees, not what he predicts.*

A particular delta neutral strategy, such as a butterfly spread, may be used in one situation with Google, based on the trader's prediction of a sideways price channel. Perhaps Google has announced earnings and traded to about $600 per share. The trader believes this is a strong area of resistance and predicts Google will trade sideways around $600 for the next two weeks. He establishes a butterfly spread centered on $600 with the current month options. This is directional trading, based on the trader's analysis and prediction of the future price movement of Google. He is using a delta neutral trade, but this trade is based on the trader's prediction of Google's price remaining close to $600 per share.

By contrast, the non-directional trader may be using a butterfly spread on the Standard and Poor's 500 Index (SPX) every month, using a well defined set of trading rules to manage this trade. This trader is not predicting SPX will trade sideways; he has established a set of rules that determine how he will react to the price movements of SPX from day to day. He tries his best not to predict tomorrow's price movement; he only reacts to the price move he sees in today's market. The non-directional trader's plan is to manage the risk of the trade with timely adjustments and benefit from the time decay inherent in the options.

This distinction in delta neutral trading and non-directional trading may seem semantic at first blush, but I emphasize the distinction for good reason. The non-directional trader who has developed his trading system may be tempted at some point in the trade to deviate from his system's rules. His trading system may dictate that an adjustment is required if the index breaks a certain price level. If the trader is following his system with discipline, he will make the adjustment promptly without delay. However, if he analyzes the markets and external factors and concludes that the market will pull back in a couple of days, he may decide the adjustment isn't necessary. This trader has now poisoned his trading system! He is mixing price predictions within a system designed for the directionally agnostic trader. It is a common trap that the non-directional trader may fall into – he predicts the adjustment isn't needed; the market continues to move against him and he eventually takes a much larger loss as a consequence.

The non-directional trader tries his best not to predict where the market is going tomorrow. Instead, he focuses on where the market is today and the actions his rules dictate. He follows the rules. This may seem like a fine distinction in semantics, but give it a try. You will find yourself shedding a lot of stress as you simply focus on what the market is doing today and what your rules dictate.

Summary

The phrase, delta neutral, has often been used as a buzzword to market and sell options trading systems, newsletters and options education. As a result, considerable confusion and misunderstanding surrounds the concept of delta neutral trading strategies.

A delta neutral trade is an options position with minimal risk associated with the price movement of the underlying stock or index. We may use a delta neutral trade in two distinctive situations:

➢ The directional trader uses a delta neutral trade to profit from her prediction that the underlying stock or index will trade within a narrow, sideways channel for the duration of the trade. This trade is based upon the trader's analysis of a specific stock or index and the overall market environment, and her prediction of minimal future price movement.

➢ The non-directional trader uses a delta neutral trade with a trading system of rules that guides the trader's response to market movement up, down, or sideways. No prediction of the future price movement of the underlying stock or index is made within this strategy. This trade is replicated month after month as an income generation strategy.

The directional trader may use a delta neutral trading strategy when she has predicted a sideways price movement. The non-directional trader makes no prediction about future price moves; he is simply trading delta neutral strategies with a set of rules dictating his trade adjustments based on the most recent market move. It is crucial that the non-directional trader trades his system with strict discipline and does not slip into predicting the market's future price moves. Trading delta neutral, either directionally or non-directionally, requires a robust system of risk management for long-term success.

CHAPTER TWO

WHY DO PROBABILITIES MATTER?

Many years ago, I was sitting in an options trading class, and the slide being used in the class had been copied out of an options analysis software program. The classic risk/reward curve for the options position had been drawn, showing the ultimate gains or losses for different values of the stock price at option expiration. The software had also printed the probabilities of the underlying stock closing at various prices at expiration. The instructor told us to "ignore the probabilities on the chart". He was a classic stock picker who used options as his trading vehicle once he had a bullish or bearish stock candidate. But he didn't understand how options were priced; he considered the probability calculations irrelevant.

Experienced option traders know that one of the fundamental factors determining the price of an option is the probability of that option expiring with tangible value, i.e., what we option traders call *in the money*, or ITM. So probabilities do matter to the options trader and the probability calculation is a valuable tool that we will use to evaluate competing trade candidates and to position our income generation trades with consistent risk month after month.

Who Was Gauss?

Carl Friedrich Gauss was a mathematician and scientist who lived in the early part of the nineteenth century. His achievements in mathematics and several areas of science and engineering were quite significant. One of his comparatively minor achievements was the normal distribution in statistics, often called a Gaussian distribution in his honor. You may not be familiar with a Gaussian distribution, but I would venture that you have heard of the "Bell Shaped Curve", the Gaussian distribution by another name. In fact, the German government honored Gauss with his portrait and a Gaussian distribution curve on the ten Deutsche Mark banknote from 1989 through 2001.

The Gaussian distribution, also known as a normal distribution, is sometimes referred to as a probability distribution because of its use in predicting the probability of a data point being found within the distribution. Figure 2.1 depicts the distribution of body weights for a group of men; this is an example of a classic probability distribution curve.

Figure 2.1
A Probability Distribution Curve

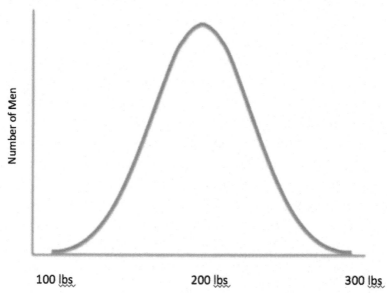

This curve represents all of the data in what might be called a data set or a population of data, in this case, all of the individual weights of the men. The height at any particular spot on the curve corresponds to the probability of the occurrence of a datum with that value in the population, i.e., a man with that weight. Thus, as we move toward either extreme of the curve, those values have a low probability of occurrence. If we walked into the room of these men blindfolded, the probability of touching a man weighing 250 pounds or more is relatively small, but the probability of touching a man weighing about 200 pounds is relatively high.

An example will illustrate how we might use the probability distribution in a practical application. Assume we are throwing a pair of dice and each die has six sides with a number of dots on each side, signifying the numbers one to six. If we work through all of the possibilities, we find that the smallest number we can roll is a two with each die coming up with the number one and the largest number is a twelve with a six on each die. There is only one combination of the dice that can produce a twelve and one combination that can produce a two. But there are six combinations that may produce a seven and several other combinations for the numbers three through eleven. We have displayed these possibilities in Figure 2.2, and we see a pattern similar to what we saw in the normal distribution curve.

Figure 2.2
Probability Distribution For Two Dice

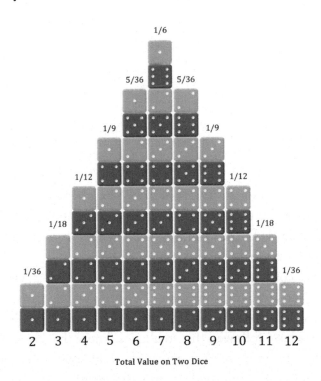

Total Value on Two Dice

This resulting probability distribution shows us that the number seven is the most probable result of our throwing the dice. There is a one in six chance of throwing the seven or about 17%. If I start throwing the dice and keep track of the results, what I will find is that the data will slowly converge to that 17% value for the number of times the seven results from our tossing the dice. The probability distribution gives us very accurate predictions for the probabilities of any number resulting from our dice throw, assuming we throw the dice a large number of times.

We can apply this same reasoning to the probabilities of future prices for a stock. An example is illustrated in Figure 2.3.

Figure 2.3
Probability Distribution For A Stock Price

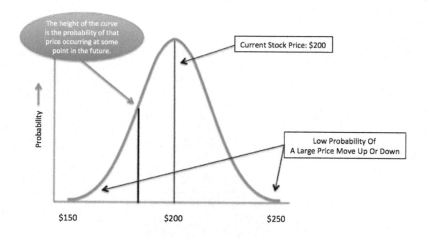

The peak of the probability distribution is at the current stock price. As we know intuitively, the probabilities are highest for small moves up or down in price and the probabilities are smallest for either a very large increase or a very large decrease in the stock price.

Statisticians compute what is known as the standard deviation for a set of data; this statistical measure quantifies how widely dispersed the data are. Imagine if the stock price distribution in Figure 2.3 was for General Electric. If you have followed this stock, you know that the stock price has stayed rather constant for years, with relatively small price changes each day. Thus, our calculation of the standard deviation for General Electric will be a small number and the corresponding probability distribution will be tall and narrow, similar to the curve on the right in Figure 2.4. This shows us visually that the probability of a price move of five dollars is very small. But we would see a very different probability distribution for a stock like Netflix. Netflix's stock price can easily move $10 or more in one day, so the standard deviation is a larger number. The probability distribution curve will be broad, yielding much higher probabilities for that five-dollar price move. Netflix's probability distribution curve would be shaped more like the one on the left in Figure 2.4.

Figure 2.4
The Effect Of Standard Deviation

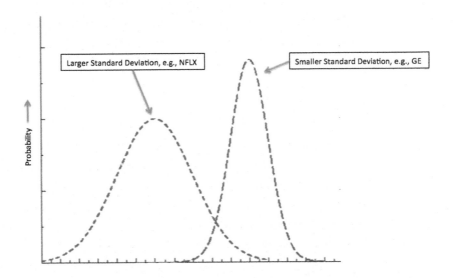

When we apply the statistics of probability distributions to stocks, we could use the historical volatility of the stock's past price movements in place of the standard deviation. We calculate historical volatility by simply averaging the absolute value of the daily stock price moves over a specified period of history. Returning to our example above, the thirty-day historical volatility for Netflix at the time of this writing is 53% and has ranged as high as 149% over the past year. By contrast, General Electric's thirty-day historical volatility is currently at 24% and has ranged as high as 48% over the past year. These contrasting values of historical volatility confirm in quantitative terms what observers of these stocks already know intuitively: Netflix can move around in price far more than General

Electric. But now we have quantified that price volatility, and can more precisely compare one stock to another.

We will discuss historical volatility and implied volatility in detail in Chapter 5. Without getting into the detail here, implied volatility is an estimate of future variation in price as opposed to the actual, realized variation in price we see from the historical prices. Since implied volatility is a forward-looking estimate of price variation, using the implied volatility in our calculations is the superior method for calculating probabilities for future price movements for our stocks. When the trader is considering the typical directional stock or options trade, she begins with a prediction of the stock price over a particular period of time. Since implied volatility is effectively the market's consensus of the particular stock's future price variation, that is the correct number to be used in our probability distribution calculation.

How Does It Work In Real Life?

At this point, you may be wondering if any of these statistical measures are of practical use to the trader. The answer is a resounding yes, but we do have to discuss the limitations of these probability calculations when applied to stock prices before we continue. We have all seen fine-sounding theoretical explanations that nearly collapse when compared to the actual measurement data from the "real world". Our probability distribution calculations are not perfect, but they remain quite useful tools for options traders.

In our earlier example with throwing dice, we saw that the probability distributions give us very accurate predictions for perfectly random events, such as throwing dice, flipping a coin, drawing a card from a deck, or predicting which number will come up on the roulette wheel. But the stock market has many non-random factors affecting stock prices. Global events such as war or disruption of an oil supply route may influence the prices of all stocks or stocks in a particular industry segment. We also observe crowd psychology at work when a rumor starts a selling or buying spree that is short lived. Unexpected events such as the sudden resignation of a company's CFO may cause a large drop in the stock price, but as more information becomes available, that price may rebound significantly.

When we compare actual stock price moves with the prices predicted from our probability distribution curve, we find a larger number than predicted for the large price moves either up or down. The probability of a three standard deviation move up or down is very small, less than 0.2% in either direction. But, in "real" life, three standard deviation moves in stock prices occur much more often than predicted by the probability distribution. This is what statisticians refer to as the "fat tails problem", i.e., the tails of the probability distribution curve on the far right and far left of the chart are higher than was predicted – the tails are fatter.

What that means for us as stock and options traders is that these probability calculations are not precise predictions of the future, but we will find that they will give us a reliable basis for our trade the majority of the time. I have not done anything approaching a scientific study, but from my experience, these calculated probabilities are reasonably accurate about 80-85% of the time. We aren't precisely predicting the future, but it beats wandering in the dark!

Calculating Probabilities

Your broker's web site probably has a probability calculator among the tools they provide for their customers. You may download a probability calculator in the free downloads section of my web site: www.ParkwoodCapitalLLC.com.

You can build your own probability calculator very easily using the normal distribution function that is built into Microsoft Excel. The probability of the stock price closing below the target price at expiration is calculated by the following formula in Excel:

Probability of Closing Below P_T = NORMSDIST{[LN(P_T / P_0)]/[(implied volatility/100)*SQRT(t/365)]}

Where:
NORMSDIST is the normal distribution function supplied by Excel
LN is the natural logarithm function supplied by Excel
SQRT is the square root function supplied by Excel

P_0 is the current price of the stock or index
P_T is the target price of the stock or index
implied volatility is the annualized implied volatility for
the stock or index
t is the time period of interest in days (often the time
remaining to expiration)

This calculation result will be in decimalized form, e.g., a probability of 45% will be calculated as 0.45. In Excel, you may format the cell for the formula result as a percentage. Since the probability of all prices must sum to 100%, the probability of the stock or index price closing above the target price is found by subtracting the formula above from one:

Probability of Closing Above P_T = 1 - NORMSDIST{[LN(P_T / P_0)]/[(implied volatility/100)*SQRT(t/365)]}

The denominator of the normal distribution term is:

(implied volatility/100)*SQRT(t/365)

This is the formula you can use to convert the annualized implied volatility value supplied on your broker's web site to any period of time desired. This formula assumes implied volatility is entered in percentage form, i.e., 35% or 35, so it first divides by 100 to convert to the decimal form of percentage. Then it is multiplied by the square root of the time period of interest in days divided by 365. Some will argue that we should divide by the number of trading days in the year instead of calendar days, since volatility by definition can only change during a trading session. That is the most technically precise answer, but, in practice, most options data sources will list days to expiration in calendar days in their options chains. So, as a matter of convenience, I use calendar days. For the retail trader, the differences are not material. Therefore, converting the annualized implied volatility to a lesser time period may be calculated as:

Implied volatility for a period of t days = (implied volatility/100)*SQRT(t/365)

Where:

implied volatility is the annualized implied volatility for the stock or index

SQRT is the square root function supplied by Excel

t is the time period of interest in days (often the time remaining to expiration)

The following examples may be of use in testing the output of your spreadsheet.

For IBM trading at $193 with implied volatility at 16.2% and 28 days to expiration, the probability of IBM closing above $200 at expiration is 21.36%.

Google's implied volatility is posted as 29.4% and this corresponds to an implied volatility of 5.96% for the next 15 days.

Using Probabilities In Options Trading

We will use probability calculations principally in two ways in our options trading:

➢ Calculating the probability of success for several trade candidates and using this information to select the best trade.

➢ Positioning the non-directional options trade to ensure a consistent level of risk exposure from month to month.

You probably noticed that implied volatility was one of the variables in the probability calculations of the previous section. If an experienced trader were comparing two options trades, one on Google that required a ten dollar move for success, and the other on Microsoft that required a ten dollar move for success, the trader would know that the ten dollar move on Google was much more probable. His experience with these stocks has taught him that Google can easily move ten or twenty dollars in one day, but Microsoft's stock price moves are typically much smaller.

The probability calculations we have discussed allow the trader to be more precise in these comparisons of different trade candidates. Whenever we establish an options trade, we may easily calculate or at least estimate the maximum gain we will achieve if the underlying stock or index moves to the price we have predicted. If we combine that maximum return with the calculated probability of success, we may calculate what is known as the risk-adjusted return, or the expected return. This is the return we might expect over time if we placed a trade similar to this one many times. We may see a large potential return for a trade, but the risk-adjusted return is a more realistic expectation of the actual return over time and many trades. Consider the following example.

IBM is trading for $199 and we buy 100 shares of stock. Then we sell one contract of the September $205 calls for $1.65. If IBM is trading above $205 at September expiration, our stock will be called away at $205 per share. So we will have a $600 gain from selling the stock at $205 plus the $165 from selling the call option, or $765. Our original investment was $19,735 (19,900 – 165), so our return is 3.9%. A four percent return in only forty nine days isn't too bad, especially if we think we might be able to do this several times throughout the year. If we calculate the probability of IBM closing above $205 at expiration, we find it is only 28.3%. Therefore, the attractive potential return is based on the unlikely prospect of IBM trading up over $6 in a little less than two months. That may give us second thoughts about this trade.

We can take this a step further by multiplying the probability of success times the maximum theoretical return to get the risk-adjusted return of 1.1% (0.283 x 3.9). This risk-adjusted return more accurately reflects the return that is likely given the probabilities of IBM trading above $205 at expiration. The risk-adjusted return is also known as the expected return because this is the best estimate of the average return over many trades if I were to establish a trade like this several times through the year.

Let's compare that trade with another covered call candidate, Priceline (PCLN), trading at $664. We sell the September $670 call for $34.80. If Priceline is trading above $670 at expiration, the position is called away from us and we have a net gain of $4,080 or 6.5%. A cursory analysis concludes that the return for a $6 move on PCLN is more lucrative than the $6 move on IBM (6.5% vs. 3.9%). PCLN's covered call return is 66% greater than the covered call on IBM. But when we calculate the risk-adjusted returns, we find an even greater difference than we thought. The probability of Priceline trading above $670 at expiration is 47.4%, which results in a risk-adjusted return of 3.1%. This risk-adjusted return is 180% larger than the risk-adjusted return of 1.1% for IBM. Each trade required a six-dollar move for success, but that didn't tell the whole story. The IBM covered call is actually a much lower probability trade, so the risk-adjusted return is rather small.

I have summarized the results of analyzing these two trades in Table 2.1. Analyzing your prospective trades in this way will give you a clearer picture of the risk. Consequently, your expectations for the results will be more realistic.

Table 2.1
Using Probability Calculations To Analyze Prospective Trades

	Stock Price	Call Strike	Call Price	Called Out Return	Probability of Success	Risk-Adjusted Return
IBM Covered Call	$199	$205	$1.65	3.9%	28.3%	1.1%
PCLN Covered Call	$664	$670	$34.80	6.5%	47.4%	3.1%

Put The Probabilities On Your Side

We will discuss the role of volatility in options trading in more detail in Chapter 5 and illustrate how options pricing is fundamentally rooted in the probabilities of the options expiring with value, i.e., in the money, or ITM. A fundamental rule of finance, regardless of the market or the financial instrument, is that greater gains will always be accompanied by higher levels of risk. We could restate that maxim in terms of the probabilities:

> ➢ A trade with a high probability of success and a low probability of loss will have a relatively low potential return.
> ➢ A trade with a low probability of success and a high probability of loss will have a relatively high potential return.

In options trading, we frequently focus on the risk/reward ratio, or the ratio computed by dividing the maximum potential loss of the trade (the risk) by the maximum potential gain (the reward). Thus, trades with large risk/reward ratios have large potential losses relative to the potential gain. Ironically, these high risk/reward ratio trades are the same trades that have high probabilities of success. Option traders have conventionally referred to the options trade with a high probability of success as the "conservative trade", and the options trade with a high probability of loss as the "aggressive trade". It is critically important to note that while the conservative trade has the highest probability of success, it also has the largest maximum loss. There is a low probability of that loss, but if the loss occurs, it will be large. The options trading strategies we discuss in this book as candidates for non-directional income trading are all relatively high probability trades, i.e., positions with probabilities of success of 60% or greater.

Consider a hypothetical options trade with a maximum potential gain of $1,550 and a maximum potential loss of $8,450. The probability of success for this position has been calculated to be about 85%. Wow! That is a high probability of success; I may be tempted to ignore the possibility of a loss. After all, I only have a 15% probability of a loss occurring.

Now let's imagine how this trade might turn out if we use it every month for a year. An 85% probability of success suggests we will collect our profit of $1,550 ten months out of the year and take our loss in only two months. That sounds pretty good, doesn't it? Our total gains are $15,500 (10 x $1,550), but our two losses tally to $16,900, so we end the year with a net loss. This illustrates the deception inherent in the high probability trade. We are encouraged by the 85% probability of success and we incorrectly assume that we don't need to concern ourselves with losses in this trade. Novice traders will often start with high probability trades, thinking that the probabilities are on their side. But that large potential loss must be considered, even though the probability of it occurring is quite small.

This example isn't an unusual or exceptional case. We have illustrated two critical characteristics of options trading:

High probability options trades always have large risk/reward ratios.

All options strategies lead to a long-term risk adjusted return near zero.

Technically, the options strategies should lead to a net return approximately equal to the cost of capital. But trading commissions and bid/ask spread slippage will often drive that net result near zero or even negative. The reason this is true is simply that the options are priced based on their underlying probabilities of expiring ITM. So there is no advantage to taking either side of the trade. We would see precisely the same results if we looked at low probability trades. In those cases, many small losses will overwhelm the occasional large gain.

This result is often surprising to options trading students. Infomercials and unscrupulous sales people have led them to believe that they can be profitable in options trading as soon as they learn the secret strategy used on the exchange floors, or some such pitch. I even heard one salesman claim he had found the "holy grail" of options trading. Pay him $5,000 and join his class and he will let you in on the secret.

So how do I make money by trading options? Consider the earlier example with the trade that has a potential gain of $1,550 in the "good" months and a potential loss of $8,450 in the "bad" months. If I can minimize that potential loss to something less than $8,450, I have a chance at a net positive return for the year. The art of adjusting and managing the position so as to never take the maximum theoretical loss is the key to success. To be successful in the long term with any options strategy, one must have a well-defined and robust system of rules to manage the risk. That is why risk management is discussed in detail in the following chapter and throughout this book. Risk management is the critical success factor in non-directional options trading.

Is Trading Options Gambling?

I often hear the charge that trading options is just gambling, together with advice to stay far away. That charge is often leveled by stockbrokers in discussions with their clients who ask about options. The irony is that the same laws of probabilities govern the price movements of stocks as well as options. In my experience, stockbrokers don't have a clue about options and are just trying to keep their clients from going elsewhere. Yes, the Series 7 examination taken by stockbrokers does include a section on calls and puts, so they may remember the basic definitions of the instruments, but that is the extent of their knowledge.

Trading stocks and options are both gambling in one sense. Probabilities largely govern the outcome of both stock and options trading. Since the typical "game of chance" also depends on those same probability distributions, one could reasonably call it gambling. However, let's consider the Las Vegas casino for a moment. If you pick any random person sitting at one of the tables in the casino, you will probably find someone who is just playing the game for the excitement and has no clue about the probabilities. They are truly gambling. However, if you encounter a professional gambler, he will be very well versed in the probabilities of the game he is playing and will be doing his best to achieve a probabilistic edge.

My father was a serious poker player. As a boy, I can recall many books in his library on the game of poker. Those books had large sections on the probabilities of the game. To be sure, the ability to read people and discern their strategies is also a very important component of the game. But any serious poker or blackjack player will be able to give you a mini-lecture on the probabilities of the game and how he uses them to his advantage.

This chapter on using probabilities in options trading is analogous. The probabilities do not guarantee the outcome. The options trader understands probabilities and applies them in his trading in several ways:

➤ Understanding the basic risk/reward characteristics of the strategy he has employed, e.g., a trade with a high probability of success will have a relatively small return coupled with a low probability of the occurrence of a large loss.

➤ The options trader will use risk-adjusted return calculations to compare trade candidates and use that information to help select the final trade.

➢ The non-directional options trader uses probability calculations to ensure she establishes her trades with a consistent level of risk exposure from month to month.

➢ Risk-adjusted return calculations assist the non-directional options trader in the development of a trading system of rules that promises a probabilistic "edge".

Return to the Las Vegas casino example for a moment. All of those casino games have a probabilistic edge in the favor of the casino. Thus, over the long term with many plays, the casino is guaranteed to be the winner. The options trader can establish a very similar system for himself, giving him the probabilistic edge. That is the subject of Chapter 3.

A Zero-Sum Game?

Economists have developed what is known as *game theory*, the study of how intelligent, well informed individuals make decisions. Sometimes it is referred to as *strategic decision making*. The beginnings of game theory date back to the forties with the work of the economist, John von Neumann. Game theory was developed more extensively in the fifties and sixties and several of the Nobel prizes awarded to economists in the twentieth century included extensive work in game theory.

Game theory is a complex subject that has been applied to several disciplines of study, but one of the most common game theory discussions within financial markets is the *zero-sum game*. The essence of the zero-sum game is that whatever I gain must be matched by someone else's loss. A good example is a poker game with seven contestants in a private home so there is no house percentage taken off the top as there would be in the typical casino. The sum of money brought to the table by all participants at the beginning of the game will be equal to the sum of money taken home that evening by the participants. Of course, the distribution of those funds will likely be quite different; there are winners and losers. This is a zero-sum game, i.e., whatever was won by one participant must have been lost by one or more of the other participants.

That raises the question: is option trading a zero-sum game? In short, the answer is no. Consider a couple of examples.

Wally is bullish on Apple (AAPL), so he buys a call option on AAPL that will expire in thirty days. The market maker is on the other side of this trade; he sold Wally the call, so he is short the call and will profit if AAPL's share price declines. If the trade stayed here, it would be a classic zero-sum game; either the market maker wins because AAPL declined in price, or Wally wins because AAPL's share price rose. But market makers don't operate this way; they don't take directional positions. Market makers do their best to remain close to delta neutral on the underlying stock and make their profits based on the bid/ask spread of the options. In this example, the market maker would reduce or eliminate his risk in one of two ways. He might have the opportunity to buy that same AAPL option from another trader who wishes to sell the AAPL call. The market maker now has no position in AAPL; he has eliminated his risk. Alternatively, the market maker might choose to hedge his short AAPL call option by buying AAPL stock. Now the market maker is indifferent to whether AAPL rises or falls in price. Your option trading with the market maker is not a zero-sum game.

Consider another example. Dilbert buys Netflix stock (NFLX) and sells the call option just above the current stock price, forming the classic covered call. The market maker is now long that NFLX call. But Alice enters an order to buy a NFLX call at that same strike and expiration, so the market maker sells the option without having to hedge his position. He locks in the gain represented by the difference in the purchase and sale prices of the call option. The market maker now has his profit, independent of NFLX's future price movement. There are several possible outcomes, but consider the bullish case where NFLX trades higher and closes at expiration at a price much higher than the strike price of the call option in question. Dilbert makes a profit, but Alice also made a profit on her trade. In this example, all three market participants are winners. Option trading is not a zero-sum game.

Summary

The probability distribution function plays a fundamental role in option pricing. The Gaussian distribution is also known as a normal distribution, or a probability distribution. Many will recognize this as the famous "bell shaped curve". The formulas for building an Excel spreadsheet for calculating probabilities were included in this chapter. One may also download a probability calculator spreadsheet from the author's web site,

www.Parkwood CapitalLLC.com.

Understanding the probability distribution function is critical for option traders:

1. The probability distribution function teaches the options trader the basic risk/reward characteristics of the strategy he has employed. He knows that a trade with a high probability of success will have a relatively small return coupled with a low probability of the occurrence of a large loss. And conversely, the trade that promises a huge potential return will carry a low probability of success. But the low probability trade has a relatively small maximum loss, albeit with a high probability of occurrence.

2. Option traders know that option pricing is inherently based on the probability of that option having value at expiration. It follows that there is no advantage to taking either side of the trade. The options trader develops a probabilistic edge by following strict risk management rules so the maximum potential loss of a trade is never realized.

3. The options trader will use risk-adjusted return calculations to compare trade candidates and use that information to help select the optimal trade.

4. The non-directional trader will use the probability distribution function to establish his positions month after month with a consistent level of risk. When coupled with a robust system of risk management, this results in a sound non-directional trading system. Probability calculations are one of the tools used by the non-

directional trader to consistently apply his trading system rules month after month.

The options trader uses the probability distribution calculations to ensure that the trading system he has developed has a probabilistic edge. Options trading does carry a risk of loss; in that sense, one might consider it gambling. If the options trader carefully develops the probabilistic edge, then he is more akin to the casino rather than the gambler at the tables in the casino.

Several examples in this chapter demonstrated that the retail options trader is not engaged in a zero-sum game with the market maker or other traders. This naturally leads us to the subject of the next chapter, risk management. It is only through a robust system of risk management that the options trader may enjoy an edge in his trading.

CHAPTER THREE

THE SECRET OF OPTIONS TRADING

We have all seen the marketing material and infomercials designed to sell trading software, training courses, coaching, DVDs, books, and other products and services for trading and investing. Many times the claim is made that this is the "secret strategy" used on the exchange trading floors to make fortunes. I once heard the speaker in a webinar actually say he had traded for several years before discovering "the Holy Grail" of options trading. Of course, his purpose was to sell his trading system; to the degree that he can convince the listener that he has discovered the secret or the Holy Grail, he will be successful in selling his system. In the sense that all of these sales people are promoting, I can assure you that there is no secret, or Holy Grail, to options trading. But there is a secret to being successful in options trading and it is rather simple: MANAGE YOUR RISK.

The Lowly Stop Loss

Why is the stop loss order so underutilized? To a large degree, I think traders do not want to think about the possible loss. We are focused on our analysis and "being right". All stockbrokers offer the trailing stop loss order, which may be configured to trip if the stock price pulls back a specified dollar amount or a specified percentage. Imagine how many investors could have saved a large portion of the gains in their stock accounts in 2008 if they entered simple trailing stops on all of the stocks in their retirement portfolios.

I have never met a trader who didn't talk about and acknowledge the value of stop losses. Unfortunately, I have known many traders, including myself, who stayed in trades well after the stop loss they originally established was exceeded. The following are warning signs that your stop loss may not be adequate:

➢ My stop loss is just a vague number in my head.
➢ The stop loss isn't written in my trading journal at the beginning of the trade.
➢ I have multiple stop losses in mind, e.g., I have identified a 50% stop loss, but have also noted a support level on the price chart that, if broken, will be my stop.
➢ My stop loss is not entered with my broker as a contingency order to be automatically executed if the trigger criteria are met.
➢ I have frequently moved my stop loss on the basis of my analysis of the price chart, after the trade was underway.
➢ I avoid entering a stop loss order because I may get filled at an unfavorable price.

The "flash crash" of 2010 resulted in a huge debate about stop loss orders issued as market orders versus limit orders. Many stop loss orders were filled during the couple of minutes of the flash crash, and, not surprisingly, the fill prices weren't great. After all, the market appeared to be in free fall for a few minutes and then it rebounded nearly as rapidly as it fell. This resulted in many "trading gurus" lecturing anyone who would listen about the evils of the stop loss entered as a market order.

I will grant that any stop loss orders that triggered during the flash crash took people out of their positions at unfavorable prices and then those same positions recovered much or all of their value during that same trading session. That was frustrating. But drawing the conclusion that one shouldn't use a market order in one's stop loss is not the right answer. After all, the purpose of the stop loss is to salvage the trading account before irreparable damage occurs. In the crashes of October 1987, the fall of 2008, the spring of 2009, or in August 2011, the trader was thankful to be taken out of his position; the price was secondary. Stopping the bleeding was the priority. If my stop loss order was a limit order during any of those crashes, I may not have been filled at all — so my losses would not have been contained.

As in everything else in life, there is no free lunch in trading. If I use a market order within my stop loss, I will always be taken out of the losing trade. If we have another flash crash, then I may see myself taken out of the trade at a poor price and then be frustrated because the market immediately recovered. During my thirty five years of trading, the stop loss order being immediately executed as a market order has been the better move in every case except on May 6, 2010. Don't plan your stop loss based on the exceptions from history.

When positioning the stop loss for the position, consider the probabilities discussed in the previous chapter. If the probability of loss is 50% (not uncommon for an options spread positioned near the current price of the underlying stock or index), then the probability of our stop loss triggering is at least that high or higher. Therefore, I should expect to be frequently stopped out of that trade; that is the nature of that trade set-up.

The power of the simple stop loss is huge, but often overlooked.

The 200% Rule

The 200% rule is another powerful, but simple, risk management technique. It may be used whenever the trader has a credit spread or a multi-legged position made up of credit spreads, such as an iron condor. The essence of the 200% rule is this:

1. After establishing the credit spread, monitor the trade each day.
2. Whenever you see that the debit to close the position is double the original credit, close the spread.

One complicating factor should be noted. Whenever I look at my credit spread on my broker's screen, I will see an ask price which is effectively the "retail" price to close the spread. Just as when you are buying a car, it is rare to pay retail to close the spread. So I will trigger my 200% rule when my best estimate of the price to close is approximately double the original credit. This is most likely a few cents above the midpoint, or the "mark", for the spread.

The 200% rule is a very conservative, and effective, method of controlling one's risk when trading individual credit spreads or the iron condor strategy; we will discuss its use with the iron condor strategy in more detail in Chapter 13.

Adjusting the Position

Market makers make their living in a similar way to the used car salesman who buys a car at the auction at wholesale and then sells it on his lot at retail. Of course, there is a lot of haggling over the price, but in general, both the used car salesman and the market maker generate a profit from the difference between the wholesale and the retail prices. If the market maker can buy the IBM $200 call from me at $1.54 and sell it to you at $1.60, he has collected the "spread" of $0.06. One big difference between the used car salesman and the market maker is the number of transactions. The market maker has to make a lot of transactions since the profits are relatively small. So one of the measures of success for the market maker is to take as many trades as possible. Volume is essential when you are living off a small margin.

How does he monitor and control his risk? He monitors his risk with the net delta of his portfolio of long and short options. We will discuss the Greeks, including delta, in Chapter 4. For now, just understand that if the market maker's portfolio of IBM options has a large net positive delta, it is the same as owning a large stock position in IBM. So his risk is a decline in IBM's stock price. Conversely, a large net negative delta is analogous to being short a large number of IBM shares and carries the risk from a bullish rally in IBM's stock. The market maker will hedge that risk by buying IBM stock to add positive delta – this brings the net delta up to a number closer to zero and therefore, lowers his risk. Similarly, if the market maker finds himself with a large positive delta position in IBM options, he will short IBM stock to reduce his risk.

As long as the market maker hedges himself appropriately each day, his risk is controlled. If not, he won't be in business for long. Sooner or later, the market will gap open up or down several points and he will take a large loss. As we noted earlier, the market maker makes his living off the bid/ask spread. When you are making pennies from each transaction, you can't afford to suddenly take a loss of several hundred thousand dollars. It is precisely the same for you as a retail options trader. If you don't focus on controlling your risk, you won't be in business for long.

Properly managing and adjusting the non-directional trade is essential for success. But don't misunderstand. Trade management does not eliminate losses. It minimizes losses and avoids the catastrophic loss. I have examples from my own trading where I achieved a profit after multiple adjustments in an extremely volatile market, such as the mini-crash in August of 2011. But those are the exceptions; achieving a profit is unusual after adjusting one's position in those extreme markets. But minimizing the loss is quite feasible. Minimizing losses keeps you in business.

The non-directional trader manages her risk in much the same way as the market maker. The typical non-directional, or delta neutral, position starts its life with a small delta value. The trader monitors the changing risk profile by monitoring delta. When delta reaches predetermined levels, either too large a positive number or too large a negative number, the position is adjusted in such a way as to bring delta back closer to the starting point.

For each of the non-directional strategies discussed in the latter half of this book, we will discuss trade management and adjustment in detail. This is the essence of risk management. This is the secret of success for the non-directional trader.

Why Do We Have To Adjust So Often?

I have traded non-directional income generation options strategies in my personal accounts for many years and configure my trades to have a probability of success of 85% or higher. Based on that probability, one might reasonably expect to have about ten "good" months each year where I make a profit and two "bad" months where the market turns against me and I take a loss. Therefore one might expect adjustments to be relatively unusual.

However, in practice, I find my system of risk management compels me to make adjustments to my positions at least eight or nine months out of the year. In fact, I am surprised when I close a position in a month where no adjustments whatsoever were required. At first blush, that large number of adjustments appears inconsistent with a probability of success over 85%. The answer to this apparent conundrum is two-fold and the first answer lies in the probability calculation itself.

The probability we discussed in Chapter 2 is the probability of the stock or index price closing at expiration above or below a particular price level. This calculation tells us nothing about the probability of the stock or index price running up to touch the short strike price of our position and then pulling back to close below that price at expiration.

A completely different calculation is required for the *Probability of Touching*. This is a more complex calculation and requires a random number generator in the calculations to simulate random price movement up and down during the time period of interest. Often, these are referred to as Monte Carlo calculations. The probability of touching gives us the probability of the stock or index price touching the short strike price of our position at any time between now and expiration.

Intuitively, you would expect the probability of touching to be higher than the probability of closing, and it is. For example, with Google stock (GOOG) trading at $728, implied volatility at 28% and 30 days to expiration, we sell the 800/810 call spread. If GOOG closes at expiration at a price below $800, we make our maximum profit on the trade. The probability of GOOG closing at a price below $800 at expiration under these circumstances is 89%. Looking at this example another way, we would say the probability of GOOG closing above $800 is only 11%. This is the classic high probability trade. But when we calculate the probability of touching, we get a different story. The probability of GOOG's stock price touching $800 at any time between now and expiration is 24% - over twice as high a probability as we were thinking!

Thus, part of the answer to the question of why adjustments are so common even on high probability trades is that the probability of touching is much higher than the probability of closing. The index or stock price may run up or drop down and threaten our position but then pull back to close at the lower or higher price. A reliable rule of thumb for the probability of the price of the underlying stock or index price touching your short option position is that it is very close to twice the probability of closing ITM. On this basis alone, we would expect to adjust or hedge our high probability trades more often than expected from the calculated probability of closing.

But there is another factor at work requiring us to adjust more often than predicted by the probability of closing. One of the fundamental characteristics of the high probability options strategy is a relatively large risk to reward ratio. This strategy has a high probability of success and a low probability of loss, but if the loss occurs, it will be large. The only way this strategy is feasible over the long term is if we minimize the losses when the market moves against us.

Risk management systems reflect the risk profile of the trader; some systems are designed to adjust the position sooner; others wait longer before hedging the position. Triggering the adjustment earlier will result in a smaller loss if the index or stock price continues to move against us. But this approach will result in many situations where the index or stock price moved against our position, triggering our adjustment, but then the index or stock price pulled back and we removed the adjustment. Adjustments are analogous to insurance – there is a cost for the insurance even though the risk did not materialize. Risk management systems that adjust earlier will sacrifice some of their gains over the long term, but will avoid the larger losses. This is analogous to an insurance policy with a small deductible and a larger premium. On the other hand, risk management systems that delay the hedge will adjust less frequently, but may incur a larger loss from time to time. Continuing the insurance analogy, this is the policy with a smaller premium but a large deductible.

In either case, whether we adjust earlier or later, we will always be adjusting well before the underlying index or stock price comes anywhere near our position. So the second reason we will see more frequent adjustments than the probabilities suggest is that the prudent trader hedges the position at the earliest sign of trouble, not after the truck has run over him.

Novice options traders often seek out the high probability trading strategies because they think these trades will be more conservative. In one sense, that is true. The probabilities are on the trader's side. But when a conservative investor buys thirty-year treasury bonds, he knows this is a relatively safe investment that doesn't require close attention. That is certainly not true of the high probability options trade. There is a large potential loss for the high probability options trade, but its probability of occurrence is small. Management and adjustment of the trade are essential to its long-term success.

Money Management

I commonly use the term, risk management, in two distinct contexts. Risk management is the rule or set of rules that control the downside risk for any particular trade. But I also use risk management as the umbrella phrase to cover the management of risk for the entire investment portfolio. The concept of constricting the risk of a single trade within a portfolio to a relatively small percentage of the overall portfolio is often called *money management*.

The essence of money management is determining a maximum potential loss that may be incurred on any single trade. The specific percentage chosen for the money management rule is subject to the trader's personal risk profile. In my experience, most traders use a relatively small percentage, often between 1% and 5%. For example, if I specify 3% as my money management guideline, I will evaluate the risk in any prospective trade and determine the worst-case scenario, i.e., what is the likely loss if my stop loss kicks in and I close the position? If that potential loss exceeds 3% of the total portfolio, then I will either scale back the position or not place the trade. A few examples will prove helpful.

$50,000 Portfolio Trading Covered Calls

1. Sue sets her money management guideline at 2% or $1,000 per trade.
2. She sets a contingent stop loss order to close each covered call position if the stock price pulls back 7%.
3. Sue is considering a covered call on QCOM. She estimates a loss of $362 if the stop loss triggers on a position consisting of 100 shares of stock and one short call option contract.
4. She divides the potential loss into $1000 to determine the number of shares of QCOM: 1000/362 = 2.76. Therefore, Sue buys 300

shares of QCOM and sells 3 contracts of calls to create the position.

5. If the QCOM trade moves against Sue, her realized loss should be approximately 2% or less of her portfolio value.
6. Sue will follow this process for each trade within this portfolio to limit the loss on any one trade as a percentage of the overall account balance.

$50,000 Portfolio Trading Iron Condor Spreads

1. Chris sets his money management guideline at 5% or $2,500 per trade.
2. Chris trades two sixty-day iron condor positions, one in the front expiration month and one in the next expiration month.
3. His risk management system has consistently held his losses to under $200 per condor in any given month.
4. Chris would trade 13 contracts per condor (2500/200 = 12.5) to ensure that the losses in any given month would be less than 5% of the portfolio value.

$50,000 Portfolio Trading Vertical Spreads

1. Ray sets his money management guideline at 3% or $1,500 per trade.
2. He sets a contingent stop loss order to trigger at the break-even price of the spread for each position.
3. When considering a prospective trade, Ray estimates the loss for one contract if the stop loss is triggered (a rough estimate using an options calculator).
4. Ray determines the number of contracts to be used in the trade by dividing the estimated loss into the 3% money management value of $1,500, e.g., he estimates the loss on a prospective GOOG credit spread if the stop triggers to be $345 for one contract; Ray will sell 4 contracts of the GOOG credit spread (1500/345 = 4.3).

As you can see from these examples, the basic steps to employ effective money management principles are:

1. Determine the maximum loss in dollars that you are willing to tolerate on any single trade.
2. Compute the percentage of that loss figure in terms of the total portfolio balance.
3. Analyze the proposed trade at the smallest possible size, usually one contract, and estimate the expected loss if the stop loss is triggered.
4. Divide the expected loss into the maximum loss from step one above. This gives you the maximum number of contracts that may be used in the prospective trade without violating your money management rules.
5. As the account grows, use the percentage calculated in step two to update the maximum loss figure.

The reader may have noticed one flaw or "weak link" in the money management process outlined above. The trader needs to estimate the expected loss for the trade if it goes against him. In the case of simpler trades, such as a vertical spread with a contingent stop loss order, that may be reasonably straightforward. However, on more complex non-directional trades, such as the iron condor spread, that estimated loss depends heavily upon the trader's adjustment system and her skill at managing the trade. I point this out to emphasize the importance of that loss estimate; if in doubt, err on the conservative side and trade a smaller position. As the trader gains more experience with a particular strategy, the accuracy of those loss estimates will improve.

The basic principle of money management can be illustrated in another way. Human beings are generally optimistic and thus traders normally focus on the maximum gains when establishing a trade. Money management principles force the trader to ask himself two fundamental questions:

➢ What is the worst possible outcome for this trade?
➢ Can I live with that?

If my answer to the latter question is even somewhat negative, I either need to make sure I have hedged the trade in such a way as to ensure that a smaller loss is the maximum loss possible, scale back the size of the trade, or not enter the trade at all. Robust risk and money management rules, and the discipline to follow them, are the foundation that ensures the trader will continue to be in business for the long term.

Summary

Risk management is the most important consideration in options trading, but it is frequently overlooked. Often it is minimized because the trader naturally doesn't want to think about being wrong. In addition, stop losses simply aren't sexy. Traders find it much more interesting to study the newest strategies or adjustment techniques. The simplest stop loss may be deployed as a contingency order placed with your broker. When the trigger price has been tripped, the order is automatically sent to the floor as a market order for immediate execution.

The 200% rule is a conservative stop loss technique for a vertical credit spread and may also be used to control the risk in the iron condor strategy (Chapter 13). The 200% rule is triggered when the debit to close the spread exceeds twice the original credit received to enter the spread.

Some trading strategies are amenable to a variety of adjustment techniques when the trade is moving against us. But don't be deceived; often, the best alternative is to simply close the trade and take the loss.

High probability options strategies often require frequent adjustments and some traders find that surprising. The explanation is two-fold:

1. The probability of touching is about twice as large as the probability of closing, so the probability of the index moving up or down far enough to touch our short strike is higher than we think.
2. The risk/reward ratios of high probability trades are large, so the emphasis of the trader on risk management is imperative. The trader must initiate her adjustment far in advance of the index price actually touching her spread.

Money management is a subset of risk management that addresses the maximum loss for any single position that the trader has established for his overall portfolio or trading account. He uses that figure to properly size the trades that make up the portfolio. When in doubt, use a smaller number of contracts.

CHAPTER FOUR

IT'S GREEK TO ME

Sometimes students are intimidated by the option Greeks. I have observed options educators make the Greeks sound more mysterious to convince traders to employ their services. But the option Greeks are reasonably straightforward, and are very powerful tools for the trader to analyze trade candidates and manage ongoing trade positions. The Greeks have all been calculated for us on our broker's web site, so the mathematics should not pose a barrier. In this section, I will present sufficient background of the Greeks for the trader to analyze and manage his non-directional trades. For those who wish to delve into this subject in greater detail, I recommend Dan Passarelli's book, *Trading Option Greeks*.

What Are the Greeks?

When corporate management is presented the proposal for a project involving a large capital investment, there is always a section of the proposal titled *sensitivities*. That section will detail how the profitability of the project will be affected if critical factors, such as oil prices or interest rates, shift during the lifetime of the project. We have a parallel situation with option positions. Changes in the underlying stock or index price will affect the profitability of the position. But option trades also have sensitivities to implied volatility, time and interest rates. The option Greeks allow us to separate out those effects so we will know which factor may present the greatest risk to the success of our trade. This allows us to more intelligently position, monitor and manage our trade because we now know the risk factor that is most critical to the success of our trade.

The oldest model for calculating the theoretical price of an option is the Black-Scholes equation. You may see other models on your broker's web site or in options analysis software, but the differences are relatively minor and irrelevant for our purposes. The Black-Scholes equation computes the theoretical price of an option based on several variables, including the price of the underlying stock or index, the strike price of the option, volatility, time and interest rates. The Greeks are quantitative measures of the sensitivity of the option's theoretical price to the several variables in the Black-Scholes model. Whenever we have an equation with multiple variables or unknown values, we often want to know how much the value of the equation will change if we hold all of the variables in the equation constant except the one of interest.

Consider the equation that describes the path of a man being shot out of a cannon at the circus. That equation will have several variables that affect the outcome: muzzle velocity of the man leaving the barrel, the man's weight, wind speed and direction, gravity, and other variables. We will be interested in knowing how far the man will travel if we vary the powder load so as to increase the initial muzzle velocity. Differential calculus will enable us to hold the other variables constant and derive an equation that will show us how the man's travel will depend on the initial muzzle velocity. Engineers use these mathematical techniques to optimize designs of a variety of products.

We may use the same mathematics to determine the sensitivity of our calculated option price to changes in the individual variables of the Black-Scholes equation, such as the stock price, while holding all other variables constant. Don't panic if your calculus is rusty. All of the math has been done for you. These mathematical derivatives are called the Greeks in options trading because a Greek letter is used to represent them.

Let's look at the big picture first before diving into the details of the Greeks. Consider the relationships of the variables in the Black-Scholes equation in broad qualitative terms. The larger the separation between the current stock price and the strike price, the smaller the option's price will become. Recalling the probability distribution's shape, this makes sense. There is a smaller probability of a price's occurrence as we move away from the peak of the distribution. This relationship of the option price and the stock price will be represented in quantitative terms by the option Greek, *delta* (Δ), and will be discussed later in this chapter.

We would expect the price of an option to increase as we have more time available for our prediction to come true. In general, longer-term options will be more expensive. This relationship of time to the price of the option is represented by the option Greek, *theta* (θ). Theta measures the change in the option price due to the passage of one day of time while all other variables are held constant. Theta values for individual options are always negative. As we have less time for the option to gain in value, or move "in the money", or ITM, the option loses value. Whenever we own an option, or are "long" an option, the option's value will decrease over time as long as other variables, such as price, remain constant. We call this time decay. If we are long options, time decay is working against us. But if we have sold options, we are said to be "short" options, and then time decay is working in our favor. In this case, our short option position will increase in value over time as long as other variables, such as price, remain constant.

If we were considering the purchase of an option on a stock that is highly volatile with frequent large price moves, we would not be surprised to find that this option was more expensive than the option of a slow moving blue chip stock with a lesser volatility. This relationship of volatility to the option price is represented by the option Greek, *vega*. Highly volatile stocks have more expensive options. Vega is unique among the Greeks in that it is not actually a Greek letter. Most commonly it is represented by a capital V. It appears that the term, vega, was just created to look and sound like a Greek letter that stands for volatility. But the source of the vega nomenclature is unknown. The academic financial literature most often uses Kappa (κ) as the Greek letter associated with the volatility sensitivity of the Black-Scholes equation.

Gamma (γ) is unique among the Greeks in that it measures the change in one of the Greeks with a change in the stock price; Gamma measures the change in delta with a one dollar change in the stock price. For those readers with more mathematics background, gamma is the second derivative of the Black Scholes equation with respect to price. Thus, gamma is a measure of sensitivity for delta. A large value of gamma alerts us to the fact that we are on a steeper portion of the risk/reward curve, i.e., the next dollar increase in the underlying stock or index price will result in a larger move in the option price than the last dollar increase, and consequently, a larger change in the gain or loss of our position. Some find it helpful to think of delta as the speed and gamma as the acceleration, or the rate of change of the speed. Thus, as gamma increases, our risk due to a price move is also increasing.

Rho (ρ) measures the sensitivity of the option price to changes in the interest rate. Generally, changes in interest rates have a negligible effect on the commonly traded options of a few weeks or months in duration. So we won't spend any time on rho in this book. Traders of LEAPS, or long-term options, must concern themselves with possible interest rate changes and the effect on their option positions. But the options trader who uses weekly and monthly options in his trading is rarely exposed to risk from interest rate changes.

Individual Option Greeks vs. Position Greeks

New options traders often confuse the Greeks associated with an individual option with the Greeks of a position consisting of several options, e.g., three long contracts of the April XYZ call options versus an XYZ spread containing long and short options, or a portfolio that holds a variety of XYZ options, long and short, in multiple expiration months. The examples in Table 4.1 should illustrate the distinctions. The options data in Tables 4.1 and 4.2 are for IBM on September 26, 2012 with IBM trading at $204 per share.

When we are computing the Greeks for a position consisting of several different options, remember the following rules:

1. Multiply the individual option Greek by the number of contracts and the 100 multiplier (as in 100 shares per contract).
2. When you are selling options, put a negative sign in front of the calculation.
3. If I am selling an option where the Greek is negative, e.g., theta, then I have a negative multiplied by a negative and this yields a positive result.

Table 4.1
Option Position Greeks

Position	Delta (Δ)	Gamma (γ)	Vega (V)	Theta (θ)
3 Long IBM Nov $200 calls	+$189	+$8.5	+$86	-$14
10 Short IBM Nov $200 puts	+$376	-$26	-$289	+$55
5 IBM Nov 210/205 Bear Call Spreads	-$80	-$0.9	-$15	+$3
10 IBM 190/195 210/215 Iron Condor	-$5	-$14	-$128	+$20
IBM Iron Condor Above Plus 2 Long Jan $200 Calls	+$114	-$10	-$40	+$13

Table 4.2 contains the individual Greeks for the IBM Nov 205 and 210 calls. The bear call spread in Table 4.1 was created by buying the Nov 210 call and selling the Nov 205 call. The position Greeks for the five November bear call spreads were calculated from the individual option Greeks as follows:

$$\text{Delta} = 5 \times 100 \times (0.32 - 0.48) = -\$80$$
$$\text{Gamma} = 5 \times 100 \times (0.0297 - 0.0316) = -\$0.9$$
$$\text{Vega} = 5 \times 100 \times (0.27 - 0.30) = -\$15$$
$$\text{Theta} = 5 \times 100 \times (-0.041 - (-0.047)) = +\$3$$

The trader will never have to manually calculate the position Greeks for a prospective position. It will be done for you in your broker's web site or in your options analysis software. However, from my own personal experience, it was helpful to work through a few examples manually. I believe that process helps one better understand the relationships.

Table 4.2
Individual Option Greeks

Position	Delta (Δ)	Gamma (γ)	Vega (V)	Theta (θ)
One IBM Nov 210 call	+0.32	+0.0297	+0.27	-0.041
One IBM Nov 205 call	+0.48	+0.0316	+0.30	-0.047

Also note one other possible area of confusion. If one of my trading buddies has the same iron condor in play as I do, we may compare our position Greeks and find they are quite different. If he has 10 contracts of the iron condor, but I have sold 17 condors, then my position Greeks will be uniformly larger by the 17 to 10 ratio – remember that the first term in our calculations was the number of contracts. Even if we have the same number of contracts, we may observe minor discrepancies; the Greeks in his broker's web site may be derived from an options pricing equation, such as Black-Scholes, that is slightly different from the one used by my broker.

Traders often trigger the adjustments of their positions from the position delta exceeding a specified value, e.g., greater than +$100. That is a valid methodology because the position delta yields the best estimate of the price risk. If my position delta = +$250 and the index drops by $10 tomorrow, my position's profit and loss will be reduced by $2,500. If that represents too much risk, then the delta trigger for the adjustment should be a smaller number. But remember that the position delta is proportional to the position size (number of contracts). So my delta trigger may not equal your delta trigger. If I am using the delta of the short option in my spread as the adjustment trigger, then we may compare our adjustment activities easily since the total number of contracts in the position is no longer relevant.

Which Trade Is Best In This Market?

The importance of the Greeks for the options trader is based on two critical uses of the Greeks:

1. Given the current conditions of this market and my predictions for this stock or index, which of these trades presents the optimal risk profile? The Greeks help us answer this question and select the optimal trade for the situation.

2. Once we have opened the trade, market conditions change; price, volatility and time all move. We will use the Greeks to monitor how our risk is changing and, perhaps even more importantly, to determine how we might adjust the position to return the risk to a level more in keeping with our comfort level.

Options trading strategies all have differing risk profiles, i.e., they have different options Greeks. Let's return to Table 4.1 and see what information we can derive from the Greeks for those positions.

First, consider the position deltas. The largest positive number is the most bullish position and conversely for the largest negative delta. The short put position is the most bullish by far with a position delta of +$376, i.e., if IBM increases by just one dollar, this position gains $376 in value. Conversely, that same one-dollar price increase would cause a loss of $80 in the bear call spreads. Notice the iron condor with a small delta value; we call this a "delta neutral" position, i.e., a change in the price of the underlying stock, IBM, will not result in much of a change in this position's value. If we were concerned that IBM was about to rally strongly, we could adjust this position by buying some long calls. Note how the addition of the January calls moves the position delta to +$114. We have adjusted the iron condor position to be more bullish. If the price of IBM moves up, the loss for the condor will be partially hedged by the addition of the January calls.

The position gammas for these trades are all relatively small, except possibly for the short put position. Gamma increases as we move closer to expiration and as the strike price of the option is closer to the current stock price. This is the reason you often hear option traders advocate closing positions on the Friday before expiration week. During expiration week, large gammas are warning us that the trade's value could move rapidly with a price move of the underlying stock or index. Large volatility shifts are another risk that is exacerbated during expiration week.

Traders often discuss the vega risk of a prospective trade. Position vegas can be positive or negative. The large negative value of vega for the short put position tells us that we are exposed to an increase in volatility – the positive change in volatility multiplied by a negative vega results in a negative price change in the overall position. But a decrease in volatility will add value to the position. In future chapters, we will discuss the vega risk of several non-directional trading strategies; the largest positive vegas are found in the ATM calendar and double calendar spreads. A decline in volatility will destroy the profitability of those trades.

The position theta is always negative for the trader holding long options, as we see in Table 4.1 with the long IBM calls. When we are long calls or puts, we have predicted a directional move for the underlying stock price. If the stock price just trades sideways and volatility remains constant, a long option position will slowly lose value due to time decay. Thus, these positions always have a negative position theta. But we see several positions in Table 4.1 with positive thetas. This occurs when we are short options as in the short Nov $200 put position, or when we have sold options with larger thetas than the options we bought, as in the IBM iron condor.

Generally speaking, when we trade non-directionally, our positions are positive theta positions that are benefiting from time decay.

Time Decay: Your Profit Machine

The option Greek, theta, tells the trader how much a given option position will gain or lose with the passage of time. Non-directional trading strategies are always positive theta positions. The position is gaining value from the passage of time.

Most of us come to options trading from a background in stock trading. The stock trader studies the fundamental aspects of the company's business, examines the stock price chart and considers various technical indicators. He determines that XYZ stock is going to rise from the current price of $123 to $150 over the next thirty days. So he buys XYZ and waits for the price move he has predicted. Thirty days later, XYZ is trading at $125; the trader isn't losing money, so he decides to give it more time. Thirty days later, XYZ is trading at $122, but the trader believes his analysis of this stock is still correct, so he holds. His waiting on XYZ to move isn't really costing him anything other than the opportunity cost of leaving his money tied up in this stock position.

Options trading is fundamentally different. Consider the same scenario, except that the trader buys a thirty-day $125 call option on XYZ. As the stock slowly trades sideways and slightly upward during those thirty days, he will watch his call option lose value. Just before expiration, with XYZ trading at $125, his call will be worth much less than the purchase price. The value of an option primarily depends on three variables: 1) the stock price, 2) the implied volatility of the option, and 3) the amount of time left before expiration. If the stock price and the implied volatility of XYZ's options remain constant, the call option will lose value as time passes. We call this time decay. Options are a decaying asset. If the stock price prediction doesn't occur in the time frame predicted for the move, the option trader will lose money on his option trade. When trading stocks, I can afford to wait for my prediction to be proven correct, but in options trading, my prediction of price and the timing of the price move must be correct.

What if I take the other side of this trade? If I sell the option, time is now on my side. If the stock price doesn't move (and volatility remains constant), I will be able to buy back that option for less than I sold it, locking in a profit. The iron condor is one of several options strategies that benefits from the passage of time. Time decay is the source of the iron condor's profits. In a more general sense, time decay is the profit basis of all of the non-directional trading strategies. Hence, the title of this book: Time Is Money.

Figure 4.1 plots the decay of the time value of an ATM (at the money) option as we near expiration. Note that the loss of value is accelerating as expiration is coming closer. Time decay in the last 30 to 45 days isn't linear, i.e., the value lost to time decay each day is growing larger. This is representative of the time decay of the ATM options in the butterfly spread or the short options of the ATM calendar spread. A similar plot of the time decay of OTM options would show more linear decay, i.e., the value lost each day would be closer to a constant value.

Figure 4.1
Time Decay Of Options

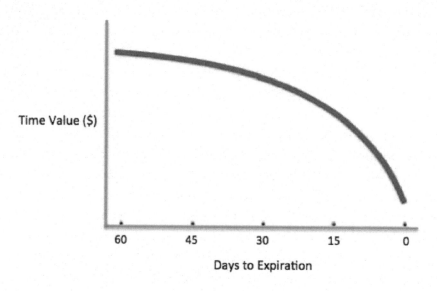

All of the non-directional trading strategies we discuss in the balance of this book are positive theta positions. Time is our friend in these trades. The time decay of those options forms the basis of our profitability. When we are trading non-directionally, time is our friend. The trick is managing the trade as the market fluctuates back and forth so that we ultimately generate a profit. The management of the trade is the secret of success for non-directional trading and the option Greeks serve as our guide.

Managing the Trade With the Greeks

As we discuss several non-directional options strategies later in this book, we will discuss the adjustment and hedging techniques the trader may use to control his risk in each of those strategies. The position Greeks are the "dashboard" we will use to monitor the position and the changing risk profile.

The non-directional options strategy always starts out delta neutral, i.e., we are not making any prediction about the market's direction. So the delta values will be small; for example, the position delta of a typical iron condor twenty-contract position will usually start out as a number less than $25 and may be positive or negative. As the underlying index begins to trend up, the position delta will trend toward larger negative numbers. If the underlying index begins to trend down, the position delta will trend toward larger positive numbers. Our adjustments will take those delta values back closer to delta neutral. We have several adjustment techniques at our disposal for whichever trade we are considering and we will evaluate those in detail in future chapters.

Our trade adjustments will generally be designed to move the position delta back closer to delta neutral to reduce our risk due to increasing or decreasing price movement in the underlying stock or index. A simple example might be a position on the Standard and Poors 500 Index (SPX) where the position delta has increased to +$150. A ten-dollar move downward in SPX tomorrow will cost us $1,500. One possible adjustment would be to buy some long puts. Each long put has a negative delta – it gains in value as the SPX decreases. The negative delta of those long puts will decrease the large positive delta of the overall position, thus moving the delta toward a more neutral position.

Consider the IBM iron condor in Table 4.1. When we initiate this position, it is very delta neutral with a small position delta of -$5. In the next line in Table 4.1, we see the effect on the position delta by adding two long calls; it increases to +$114. Imagine if we had entered the iron condor from Table 4.1, and over the next couple of weeks, IBM trades up in price and our position delta has moved to -$105. Buying two long January calls will add positive delta and move the position's delta back closer to roughly delta neutral – we have neutralized the price risk. To be precise, we don't know what the new position delta value is because the deltas of the long January calls will have risen in those intervening weeks. There are multiple moving parts in these option positions. As we add long call options to the condor position, we are decreasing the positive theta of the condor – remember that long options always have negative theta. And the positive theta of our iron condor is what generates our profit.

This serves as a representative example of the trade-offs we have to optimize when we adjust our non-directional trades. We will always be attempting to reduce our position delta back closer to delta neutral without sacrificing too much of our positive position theta. For our risk management dashboard, we will track delta for our non-directional position and when the position delta becomes too large (either a large positive or a large negative number), we will adjust the position as necessary to reduce our price risk while maintaining a positive position theta.

In Chapter 16, we will discuss the business of the market maker in options trading. His risk management dashboard is relatively simple. He takes as many options trades during the trading session as possible, trying to buy close to the bid price and sell close to the ask price. That difference in the prices, or the spread, is his profit. But since his profit is measured in a few cents to a few dollars per order, he cannot afford to take any large losses from the underlying stock price suddenly moving in either direction. The market maker tracks his risk by monitoring his portfolio delta. He buys or shorts stock to bring that portfolio delta back closer to delta neutral.

We learn three critical lessons from the market maker:

1. Risk management is job number one.
2. The option Greeks give us the dashboard to monitor that risk.
3. Frequent adjustments will be necessary to constrain our risk within reasonable bounds.

Summary

The option Greeks are quantitative measures of the sensitivities of our position to changes in the price of the underlying stock or index, changes in volatility, and the passage of time. Each individual option has its own set of Greeks: delta, gamma, vega, theta and rho. Any options position or even a portfolio containing many different options positions will have its own option Greeks; we refer to these as the position Greeks.

We will use the option Greeks in two ways: prospective trade analysis and trade management. The Greeks for a position reveal the sensitivities for each of the trades being considered. The trader then will select the trade that best reflects her evaluation of current market conditions, e.g., a negative vega options trade would be preferable for a high volatility environment when volatility is expected to decline.

The Greeks for a trading position serve as our dashboard to monitor changing levels of risk for this trade as time progresses. In future chapters, we will use the Greeks to trigger adjustments to reduce the risk of the trade as the market environment changes. We will also see the utility of the Greeks in performing "what if" analyses to determine the optimal adjustments for our positions.

CHAPTER FIVE

THE ROLE OF VOLATILITY

Volatility is a new concept for the stock trader who has recently discovered options trading. Options may be used within one's stock portfolio to control risk, augment income, and build stock positions at a discount to the market stock price. But two concepts are unique to options: implied volatility and time decay. Many beginning options traders have had the experience of buying a call when bullish on a stock, watching the stock price rise, but then being surprised to see the call value remain constant or decrease. Volatility is the culprit.

What Are All These Different Volatilities?

We can use the Black-Scholes equation to calculate the theoretical price of our option. Your broker's web site will have some type of "options calculator". It may or may not use Black-Scholes, but the principles are the same and all of the following analysis would be identical. We would enter the following data into Black-Scholes or another option pricing equation:

> ➢ Stock or index price
> ➢ Option strike price
> ➢ Historical volatility
> ➢ Days to expiration
> ➢ Interest rate

This calculation would result in the theoretical price for the option in question. But we may see a discrepancy between the actual market price for that option and the price we have calculated. The market price may be higher or lower than the calculated, or theoretical, option price, but more often, it is higher. The only variable in the Black-Scholes equation that might account for this discrepancy is the historical volatility. All of the other variables are factual figures – there is no debate about the stock price, which strike price is on our option, the days to expiration, or the interest rate. So the market participants must be pricing this option with an expectation of future volatility that is either higher or lower than it has been historically. We can calculate the volatility the market is pricing into this option by entering the market price of the option into the Black-Scholes equation and solving for volatility. The result is the volatility "implied" by the market price, or what we refer to as *implied volatility*. If the market price was higher than the theoretical price, then implied volatility was higher than the historical volatility. Thus, the marketplace has priced this option higher because they expect the future price volatility of this stock to be higher than it has been in the past. Thus, implied volatility is a measure of the market's consensus estimate of future volatility for this stock.

The variety of volatility terminology can be confusing; some definitions of the commonly used terms follow:

- ➢ *Implied volatility* is sometimes also called *future volatility* and is best understood as the market's consensus for the volatility of the underlying stock or index over the period of time covered by this option.
- ➢ *Historical volatility* is the actual measured volatility of the underlying stock or index price over a specified period of history, often the last three months or the last year. Historical volatility is also called *statistical volatility* by some authors.
- ➢ *Realized volatility* refers to the volatility as actually measured when the time period of the option under analysis comes to pass. For example, historical volatility equals 23% for XYZ stock and we calculate implied volatility to be 35% based on the pricing of the September ATM call option. The realized volatility is the 31% volatility actually measured in September. While the term, realized volatility, is often used in writing about options volatility, you

won't find it in any tables since it is now part of the historical volatility data.

The concept of implied volatility may be considered as arising in two equally valid ways. In some cases, option prices may be bid up because of the marketplace tug of war of supply and demand. If traders are anticipating a large move in the price of a stock, they may be buying large numbers of options and paying at or near the ask prices for those options. As in any other marketplace, stronger demand leads to higher prices for those options. Thus, the prices of those options are higher than would be predicted by the Black-Scholes equation - those options have higher values of implied volatility.

But implied volatility changes may also be understood from the market maker's perspective. If the market maker sees increasing demand for her options, she may reasonably conclude that the risk of a large price move in this stock has increased. The market maker's business consists of taking as many option orders as possible at the best prices possible. Her ideal is to buy options at the bid price and sell them at the ask price. She will frequently hedge her option portfolio by buying or shorting the underlying stock, because she wants to be close to delta neutral at all times. She doesn't want to speculate on a big move in the stock price; she wants to make her profits on all of those individual option trades – she wants to profit from the spread. Therefore, she will see increased demand for these options as a sign of increased risk and will raise her prices to compensate for those risks and to cover additional hedging costs.

Either way one wishes to look at it, the levels of implied volatility arise from marketplace supply and demand for the options.

Implied Volatility As A Measure Of Risk

We may also think of implied volatility as a measure of price risk. Consider the situation where we are evaluating an investment in two different stocks, both priced at $50 per share, but one with an implied volatility of 20% and the other at 85%. Often the so-called high momentum stocks are the stocks that attract our attention, but those invariably are also high volatility stocks. The $50 stock with implied volatility of 20% has a 68% probability of being between $47 and $53 in 30 days – a plus or minus one standard deviation move, but the one standard deviation range for the higher volatility stock is $38 to $62, four times as large a range of possible prices in the next thirty days! The investor who buys the high volatility stock must be prepared for wider swings in the price of his investment. In this example, the probability of a $3 move in the low volatility stock is equal to the probability of a $12 move in the high volatility stock.

Option prices may vary widely due to swings in implied volatility. For this reason, some traders follow a small number of stocks and track their historical fluctuation in implied volatility. They will buy options when implied volatility is low and sell options when implied volatility is high. As implied volatility returns to its norm, these option positions will tend to appreciate in value. As in many areas of life, the regression to the mean principle applies here as well. In fact, the tendency for regression to the mean is greater in volatility than in price movement. If the current level of implied volatility is well above or below the historical average of implied volatility for this stock or index, the tendency is to move back toward the average. But beware: just because implied volatility for this stock or index is historically high, that doesn't mean the implied volatility can't go higher yet. Implied volatilities for the broad market indexes were at historic highs in the fall of 2008, but they hit new highs before that correction was over.

Implied volatility is also the reason many beginning options traders are surprised when their option position loses value or remains unchanged even though the trader's prediction for the price of the underlying stock was correct. A decrease in implied volatility will cause the option price to decrease and may overwhelm the increase in the option's price due to the change in the stock price.

An extreme example of this phenomenon is the ATM straddle, where we buy the ATM call and the ATM put in anticipation of a large price move in the underlying stock, often after an earnings announcement. Typically, implied volatility is bid up in advance of the expected event, and then collapses after the event, dramatically reducing the prices of both of the options in our straddle. The price of the stock may move a relatively large amount based on the event, but the increased price of either the call or the put (the delta effect) may be insufficient to compensate for the loss in value of the other option due to the delta effect and the loss in value of both options due to the collapse of implied volatility (the vega effect). This is why traders find it difficult to profit with straddles. The prices of the options just before the earnings announcement or other event reflect the market's consensus of the expected range of price moves. The straddle buyer will profit only if the actual price move proves to be larger than what was priced into the market's consensus.

Implied Volatility Skews

It is common to see values of implied volatility ascribed to a particular stock, but stocks cannot have implied volatility – the stock's options have implied volatility. What is often posted or discussed as a particular stock's implied volatility is really a weighted average of the implied volatility values of selected ATM options. Therefore, you may see different values of implied volatility posted for a stock since the particular averaging processes from various sources may differ somewhat.

One might, as a first approximation, expect the implied volatility of the options for a particular stock to be about the same across expiration months and also across strike prices within a month. Those expectations turn out to be false. It isn't that simple.

The value of implied volatility of a particular stock's option at a particular strike price will tend to be similar across expiration months. When exceptions to this occur, we call these implied volatility skews. Usually, these skews reflect the market's expectations for some upcoming event. For example, on September 4, 2012, the implied volatility of the ATM $680 call of Google was 21.5% in September, 28.4% in October, and 25.1% in December. Implied volatility of the October call was higher because the market was already starting to anticipate Google's earnings announcement in October, and the implied volatility of those calls will continue to increase as the earnings announcement draws near. Thus, implied volatility skews of plus or minus one percentage point are relatively common. Larger implied volatility skews usually reflect the market's anticipation of an event that may affect the underlying stock's price in that particular expiration month. In the finance literature, the reader will find the variance of volatility across expiration months referred to as the *term structure* of the options chain.

Option traders often discuss the *volatility smile*, referring to the tendency of the values of implied volatility of the ATM options to be at a minimum and to rise as the strike prices move in either direction away from the current price. Based on the Black-Scholes pricing model, we would expect the values of implied volatility to be identical across the different strike prices for a given stock in a given expiration month. So the volatility smile is a "real world" phenomenon in contrast to the theory of the Black-Scholes model.

Table 5.1
The Implied Volatility Smile In SPX

Strike Price ($)	Call Implied Volatility (%)	Put Implied Volatility (%)
1300	0	23
1320	0	21
1340	9	20
1360	10	19
1380	13	18
1400	14	17
1420	13	16
1440	13	15
1460	12	15
1480	12	15
1500	11	15
1520	11	16
1540	11	17
1560	11	19
1580	12	21
1600	13	23

There are many theories of explanation for the volatility smile. The explanations that make the most sense to me are:

> OTM puts are more in demand for protection against a drop in stock or index price; higher demand drives higher implied volatility.
> ITM calls are more in demand as speculative trades, allowing the trader to place a bullish bet with less capital at risk.

If I subscribe to either explanation for the volatility smile, the corresponding options will have higher levels of volatility due to put-call parity, i.e., if the OTM puts are being driven up in implied volatility due to increased demand for protection, put-call parity will require the corresponding ITM call options to also rise in implied volatility.

This effect can be observed in the Standard and Poors Index November options (SPX) in Table 5.1 for SPX at $1456 on October 8, 2012. The volatility smile is most obvious in this particular example in the put options, with implied volatility ranging from 23% at the $1300 strike (far ITM) to a minimum of 15% ATM and then back up to 23% far OTM at $1600. In the SPX call options, the smile is shifted a bit OTM. Since implied volatility is fundamentally a function of supply and demand, you may see variations in the patterns of implied volatility from case to case. The picture perfect volatility smile often displayed in options books is rarely that perfect in real life. Some have referred to this as a volatility smirk, reflecting the different shapes of the curve.

Implied Volatility and Options Pricing

An option's market price is composed of three quantities: intrinsic or real value, time to expiration, and implied volatility. Often you will read that the option price consists of intrinsic and extrinsic value, where extrinsic value includes time and implied volatility. I prefer to separate out the effects of time and implied volatility, but, as we will see, it is difficult to precisely separate the value in the option due to time from the value due to implied volatility.

The intrinsic value of an option is the value of that option if it were exercised today. Thus, a $110 call option for Apple is worth $5 when Apple is selling for $115 because we could exercise our call to buy 100 shares of Apple at $110 per share, sell it for $115 per share, and have a profit of $5 per share. However, the market price of that call option is probably much higher than $5 because the market price also accounts for how much time is left until expiration as well as the implied volatility of that option.

A $110 call option for Apple with 17 days to expiration may be selling for $6.10, but another $110 call option for Apple with 45 days to expiration is selling for $7.15. Assuming the implied volatility of the two options is identical, the difference of $1.05 is due to the additional 28 days of time.

Continuing with this same example of Apple, the market price for the $120 call option with 45 days to expiration is $2.11. In this case, the intrinsic value is zero; if we were to exercise the $120 call and buy Apple stock at $120 while Apple is trading at $115, we would lose money. So we would not exercise the call because the intrinsic value is zero. The market price of the $120 call only consists of time value and implied volatility. If we compare the $120 call option with 45 days to expiration, selling for $2.11, to the $120 call option with 17 days to expiration, selling for $0.88, we see that the difference for the 28 days of time is $1.23. The difference in the $110 call option prices was $1.05 for the two different expirations, so the implied volatility of the two $120 call options must be different. This is an example of a volatility skew, where the implied volatility differs for two different months of options. This frequently occurs when an earnings announcement is scheduled for next month. The implied volatility of next month's options will be higher than the current month due to the market's expectations for a large price move following the announcement. But note that increased implied volatility does not suggest a particular directional move; it only suggests the increased probability of a larger price move than usual for this stock; the direction of the price move could be up or down.

Implied Volatility at the Beginning of the Trade

From this discussion of implied volatility, it isn't surprising that many traders monitor implied volatility and generally try to sell options when implied volatility is high and buy options when implied volatility is low. This is effectively the age-old adage of buying low and selling high. When implied volatility is low, options are less expensive and that favors their purchase, and conversely, favors their sale when implied volatility is high. For example, if the trader is bullish on Google, he has a choice of several strategies, but he may choose the specific strategy, at least in part, on the basis of the current levels of implied volatility for Google. If implied volatility is high, then he may favor strategies where options are being sold, e.g., covered calls or selling naked puts.

Some traders have confused this principle when dealing with vertical spreads. We will discuss vertical spreads in detail in Chapter 7, but one of the commonly repeated myths associated with options trading is:

When implied volatility is high, sell credit spreads, and when implied volatility is low, buy debit spreads.

In this section we will briefly show why that statement isn't true, but the full discussion is deferred to Chapter 7 where we discuss vertical spreads in detail.

With Qualcomm (QCOM) trading at $81 on July 8th, 2014, I could buy a QCOM Aug $80 call for $2.41 or $241 for one contract. I could then create a spread by selling the QCOM Aug $85 call for $0.53 or $53. I have created the QCOM Aug 80/85 call spread for $188. If QCOM closes at expiration above $85 per share, then the person who bought the $85 call option will exercise that call, requiring me to sell 100 shares of QCOM stock at $85 per share. But I will exercise my $80 call and buy 100 shares of QCOM at $80 per share and then use those shares to satisfy the $85 call exercised against me. So I bought QCOM at $80 and sold it at $85, and that leaves me with $500 in my account. I spent $188 establishing the trade so my net profit is $312 or 166%.

This vertical spread is often called a bull call spread, since it is built with calls and would be used when you have a bullish expectation for a stock. We may also create a bullish vertical put spread on QCOM by buying the $80 put for $1.69 and selling the $85 put for $4.82. In this case, we received more for the option we sold than the option we purchased, so we have a net cash flow into our account, or a credit of $313. For this spread, the maximum profit is attained when QCOM closes above $85 at expiration and both put options expire worthless. The original credit of $313 would then be the profit. This vertical put spread is often called a bull put spread.

Let's return to our first example of the QCOM 80/85 bull call spread. This spread could be established for a debit of $188 for one contract. The maximum loss for any debit spread is simply the original debit. The maximum profit for any debit spread is found by subtracting the debit from the value of the spread; if the two strike prices of the spread are $10 apart, the spread value is $1,000; if $5 apart, then the value is $500 and so on. For this example, the maximum profit is $312 (500 − 188) and the return is 166% (profit divided by the capital at risk or 312/188).

The QCOM 80/85 bull put spread could be established for a credit of $313 so the maximum potential profit is the credit or $313 and the potential return is 167% (profit divided by the capital at risk or 313/187).

The debit call spread has virtually the same return as the credit spread at the same strike prices, so there is no inherent advantage to using the debit spread or the credit spread to profit from your bullish prediction. The choice of a credit or a debit spread is principally one of style preference. Some prefer a credit spread because they can earn interest on the credit monies in their accounts while in the trade; another advantage of credit spreads is fewer trading commissions (assuming the spread may be safely allowed to expire worthless).

So the trader can be indifferent to the choice of the debit spread or the credit spread when volatility is extremely high or low. The myth to use credit spreads when implied volatility is high and debit spreads when implied volatility is low may be a confusion that arose out of long and short option positions. It is indeed true that one should consider buying low volatility options and selling high volatility options. If we are considering a long call or put position, we would look for options with low implied volatility because these are inexpensive options. Similarly, we would target high implied volatility options if we were considering a short call or put position. But when we are buying or selling a spread, we are both buying and selling the individual options. Thus, when implied volatility is high, the spread trader has bought an expensive option, but she has also sold an expensive option.

The level of implied volatility isn't a factor when we establish the vertical spread, but what happens if implied volatility shifts while we are in the spread? The answer takes us into the vega dependence of the vertical spread. Changes in implied volatility during the time we are in a vertical spread will affect the proportion of the profit available to us if we wish to close the trade early, but it does not affect the ultimate profitability at expiration.

We will expand our discussion of the effects of changing implied volatility on the vertical spread in Chapter 7 and also when we discuss condor and iron condor spreads in Chapter 13. Condors and butterflies are good examples of non-directional trading strategies that are constructed from combinations of vertical spreads. Consequently, we will see that the volatility effects on the vertical spread discussed in this chapter and in Chapter 7 will carry over to more complex trading strategies in future chapters.

Watch Your Vega!

We first discussed the option Greek, vega, in Chapter 4. The value of vega for each option describes its sensitivity to changes in implied volatility. Vega is always positive, i.e., when implied volatility rises, the price of the option rises. When we buy and sell options and create any combination of options, that position will have a value of vega that may be positive or negative. That value communicates the degree of risk inherent in the options position due to changes in implied volatility.

When one is trading non-directionally, the options strategies employed are typically delta neutral and risk management is focused on adjustments to pull the position delta back closer to zero. As we discuss each of the non-directional strategies in future chapters, we will discuss the risk presented by changes in implied volatility for that particular strategy. This is vega risk. When the position vega is a large positive number, the downside risk to the position is represented by a decrease in implied volatility; when position vega is large and negative, increasing implied volatility is the risk factor. In some cases, notably the calendar spreads, vega risk is significant and our risk management may focus on this parameter as much or more than delta. In other cases, vega risk is a lesser concern. When your position vega is negative you want the implied volatility to go down to help your position and when vega is positive you want volatility to go up. Be sure you fully understand the exposure of your positions to volatility changes. Don't be surprised in the midst of the trade.

Summary

Nearly all options traders come from a background of trading stocks and encounter two new concepts in options trading: time decay and implied volatility. In this section we discussed the different types of volatility and their effect on options trading positions.

Historical volatility is the actual measured volatility of the underlying stock or index price over a specified period of time. Implied volatility is an estimate of the future volatility of the stock or index and is based on the market's demand for the options. Implied volatility may also be viewed as a measure of risk. Stocks with high levels of implied volatility suggest that traders are expecting larger price moves in the near future than have occurred in the past. But no price direction should be inferred from the value of implied volatility.

The values of implied volatility of a particular stock's option at a particular strike price will tend to be similar across expiration months. When exceptions to this occur, we call these implied volatility skews. We will return to this concept of volatility skews when we discuss the calendar and double calendar spreads.

Black-Scholes and other pricing models predict that the values of implied volatility across the strike prices for a particular month's option chain should be flat or constant. Since the market crash of 1987, what is known as a volatility smile has been observed, i.e., the values of implied volatility for the far OTM and deep ITM options tend to be higher than the ATM options. The most probable explanation for the volatility smile is that the market reflects higher demand for the OTM puts as protection, thus driving up the prices, and therefore, the implied volatility of those options. The principle of put-call parity would then cause the ITM calls to also have elevated values of implied volatility.

The option Greek, vega, quantifies the effects of implied volatility changes on the value of our option or option position. Risk management for options positions may be more or less focused on vega risk, depending on the particular options trading strategy and its position vega. In Chapters 9 and 10, we will see that the calendar spread and the double calendar spread are the classic examples of non-directional trading strategies that have a strong dependence on changes in implied volatility. Thus, the calendar and the double calendar have large vega risk and that will be a principal focus of managing the risk inherent in those positions.

CHAPTER SIX

CAN WE USE WEEKLY OPTIONS NON-DIRECTIONALLY?

Weekly options have grown dramatically in popularity over the past couple of years. In one sense, you could say weekly options have been around since the Chicago Board Options Exchange (CBOE) started in 1973. After all, every stock has a weekly option at the beginning of expiration week, so the basic concept isn't new. What is new is their availability every week. Many of the index weekly options began to be offered in 2005 and 2006, but their popularity really spiked in 2010 and 2011 and spread to stocks. More than 300 stocks now offer weekly options and the list is growing. Over 35% of option trading volume on the CBOE now consists of weekly options. I am confident that both of these statements will be out of date when you read this book.

How Do Weekly Options Work?

Weekly options are created and available for trading on Thursdays every week except expiration week. During expiration week, the monthly option is effectively the weekly option for that stock or index. Those weekly options created on Thursday expire nine days later on Friday. However, there are exceptions to this process, and they are known as weekly options with extended expiration. Some weekly options are now created and available for trading several weeks in advance of their expiration date. As always, be sure you know the specifications for the option you are trading.

Options have an exercise style known as American or European. All stock options have American style of exercise, i.e., owners of that option may choose to exercise the option at any time before expiration. However,

European style options may only be exercised at expiration. Effectively, the owner of the European style option never has the choice of "exercising early". If the European style option is in the money (ITM) by even a penny at expiration, it will be exercised by the broker automatically. Most index options have European exercise characteristics, but there are notable exceptions such as OEX (the S&P 100 Index). Weekly options share the exercise characteristics of the other options within the particular stock or index options chain. Thus, the weekly options for Apple (AAPL) will have American exercise style whereas the weekly S&P 500 Index (SPX) options will have European exercise style. Check the exchange web sites for the detailed specifications for the option of interest, e.g., www.cboe.com.

Options differ in how they are settled at expiration. Stock and ETF (exchange traded fund) options settle in shares of the underlying stock or ETF. This is known as physical settlement. If I own three IBM $180 call options at expiration and IBM closes at $182 on expiration Friday, I will see 300 shares of IBM purchased in my account at $180 per share over that weekend. By contrast, index options are settled in cash. If I own two SPX $1900 call options at expiration and the settlement price is $1905, I will see $1,000 credited to my account over the weekend of expiration (2 contracts x 100 multiplier x $5 ITM). Weekly options share the settlement characteristics of their option chain, viz., weekly stock options will settle in shares of stock while weekly index options will settle in cash.

The settlement prices for all stock options, including the weekly options, are determined by the closing price of the stock on the Friday of expiration week. This is known as afternoon or PM settlement.

Determining the settlement price for index options is more complex and can be confusing. Index options may be specified as having either morning or afternoon settlement; you will sometimes see this referred to as AM settlement and PM settlement. SPX options have AM settlement and cannot be traded after the close on the Thursday of expiration week. The settlement price is determined by the opening price on Friday morning of each individual stock making up the S&P 500 index. But each stock doesn't trade immediately at the opening of the market, so the settlement price is not equal to the opening price Friday morning. The SPX settlement price is posted on the CBOE web site around noon on the Friday of expiration week.

But the settlement price for the weekly index options is not necessarily determined in the same way as the monthly index options. For example, the SPX weekly options settle at the closing price of the SPX on Friday, i.e., PM settlement, whereas the monthly SPX options use AM settlement. From the time the SPX weekly option is created, those options can be traded each day until 4:15 pm ET, just like the other SPX options. However, on the next Friday, when it expires, that weekly option cannot be traded past 4:00 pm ET and the settlement price is the closing price at 4:00 pm ET.

Some traders have been confused and believed they were trading SPX weekly options but they were actually trading the monthly option during the last week of its expiration. In most respects, this distinction is irrelevant. But the monthly SPX option is settled by AM settlement whereas the SPX weekly option is settled by PM settlement. Thus, the trader could be surprised at expiration by looking at Friday's closing price for SPX, when his SPX options will actually be settled based on the settlement price determined Friday morning via AM settlement.

Consider this example. Dilbert has developed a trading system in which he sells an OTM credit spread on the Standard and Poors 500 Index (SPX) every week. For example, he may sell the SPX 1880/1890 call spread on Monday of expiration week with SPX trading at $1865. Dilbert routinely trades the weekly SPX options that settle at the closing price on Friday (PM settlement). But on this particular week, Dilbert doesn't realize that he has sold the SPX monthly option spread with a week remaining until expiration; this week, his spread is made up of monthly options, not weekly options. SPX opens at $1884 Friday morning and trades up to $1895 within the first two hours of trading, but then trades off in the afternoon to close at $1798. Dilbert is relieved and believes his spread has expired worthless since SPX closed on Friday at $1798, but the SPX monthly options settled at $1891 (AM settlement) and the 1880/1890 call spread takes its maximum loss. That was a costly oversight!

The lesson here is to confirm all of the characteristics and specifications of the weekly options you wish to trade <u>in advance</u>. Don't risk a costly surprise later.

What Do The Greeks Tell Us?

It is critically important that the trader understand the exercise and settlement characteristics of the options he is trading. But what else is different with weekly options? One of the rules often taught to new options traders is to close their options positions on the Friday before expiration week. There are several reasons behind that rule:

➢ Large and rapid changes in the underlying stock price are common during expiration week.

➢ Large swings in volatility are common during expiration week.

➢ The price of the underlying stock may move in the last few minutes on expiration Friday, causing an option we thought would expire worthless to expire ITM (in the money), resulting in either a purchase or a sale of stock, surprising the trader.

The reasons many coaches and mentors cite, when they advise us to close our positions before entering expiration week, are all characteristics of our weekly option position. In other words, when we trade weekly options, we are knowingly taking those risks that we avoided with monthly options. That should give us pause.

We reviewed the option Greeks in some detail in Chapter 4. The option Greeks are mathematical parameters that quantify the risk sensitivities of our options position. We saw that larger values of the option Greek, *Delta*, indicate that the next price move by the stock may have a larger effect on the profit/loss of our options position. But *Gamma* tells us how quickly our position may turn against us. A larger value of gamma indicates the delta change is accelerating. We are entering a situation where the profit or loss of our position may change rapidly. Gamma is larger for options that are ATM (at the money) and gamma is larger as we approach expiration. Larger values of gamma for our option position are warning us of higher risk. This is the basic reason underlying the common rule to close monthly options positions before expiration week.

But weekly options, by definition, are always close to expiration. So weekly options have comparatively larger values of gamma, and, therefore, we should expect rapid changes in the value of our weekly option position. If our position is gaining in value, we may regard that as a great characteristic, but, if our position is losing value, we may not feel quite so positively about that increased leverage.

Table 6.1 compares the Greeks for a weekly AAPL $610 call with a monthly $610 call (This example was taken before the recent AAPL stock split). The first difference of note is the investment; the weekly call only requires us to risk $775 versus $2,465 for the monthly call. But one must remember that part of the reason the monthly call requires a larger investment is that it gives us much more time for our bullish prediction to prove correct. As always, there is no free lunch.

The weekly option has a slightly larger delta so we might expect a slight edge for the weekly if our price prediction proves correct. But look at gamma; the weekly option's gamma is three times as large as the monthly option. That tells us that the edge in delta held by the weekly option will only be magnified with each successive price move in Apple.

Table 6.1
Comparative Option Greeks

Option	Cost	Delta	Gamma	Theta
AAPL Jul Wk2 $610 Call	$775	$0.524	$2.06	$49 (6%)
AAPL Aug $610 Call	$2,465	$0.508	$0.65	$29 (0.8%)

Some traders will see the increased gamma as an advantage of increased leverage, i.e., he will make even more money if his predicted stock move is correct. But remember: leverage works both ways.

Theta is the option Greek that enumerates the loss in value of our options as time passes, assuming the price and volatility of the underlying stock or index remain constant. Time decay, or the loss in option value as time passes, accelerates as we near expiration. A weekly option has a lifetime of only a few days, so the change in the option price each day due to time decay is relatively large and is growing larger each day. The comparative data in Table 6.1 show the dramatic difference in theta. This weekly option loses 6% of its value over the next 24 hours. If Apple's stock price and volatility remain constant for one day, I will see a 6% loss in my weekly option position – and that was only for one day! I could buy a weekly option ATM on AAPL on Thursday and be surprised by the loss of value on Monday morning if AAPL is still trading near where it was on Thursday.

Table 6.2 details a comparison of the price behavior of the ATM weekly call versus the ATM monthly call for Apple stock. The trader is bullish on Apple and has decided to buy an ATM call with Apple trading at $610. The next day, AAPL trades down by four dollars or about 0.7%. The weekly option is down 29% while the monthly option is only down 6%. And this occurred in just one day!

Table 6.2
Comparative Option Price Behaviors

AAPL Jul Wk2 $610 Call				AAPL Aug $610 Call			
Date	Stock Price	P/L ($)	P/L (%)	Date	Stock Price	P/L ($)	P/L (%)
7/5/12	$610	$775 (cost)		7/5/12	$610	$2,465 (cost)	
7/6/12	$606	($222)	-29%	7/6/12	$606	($145)	-6%
7/9/12	$614	$13	+2%	7/9/12	$614	$202	+8%
7/10/12	$608	($302)	-39%	7/10/12	$608	$70	+3%
7/11/12	$598	($678)	-88%	7/11/12	$598	($390)	-16%

Another notable difference illustrated in Table 6.2 is the behavior of the two options over the weekend (July 6 was Friday and July 9 was the following Monday). On Monday, AAPL traded up to $614 and our weekly option position is now ahead by 2%. But the monthly option position has outperformed the weekly option with a gain of 8% - how is that possible? Over the weekend, two principal effects were driving our option prices, but those effects were in opposite directions. The delta of each option dictated a higher price for the option with the eight-dollar increase in Apple's stock price, and the two deltas are similar in magnitude. But time decay was pulling the prices of both options downward, and the theta of the weekly option is much larger than the monthly option (see Table 6.1). The end result is a larger gain for the monthly option because the monthly option lost less value to time decay.

Finally, notice that by the time we get to Wednesday, Apple has dropped down to $598, down 2% from where we started, but our weekly option has lost 88% of its value. The monthly option is also down, but by a much smaller amount at 16%. We could choose another example and see a similar but opposite effect if the stock price had met our predictions. The possibility of earning returns on the order of 100% in less than a week is what appeals to traders of weekly options, but it is critically important to realize that the magnified leverage of the weekly option works in both directions.

Some traders may find these characteristics exhilarating; others may find them disconcerting. The trader must determine his comfort level in advance. Don't be surprised.

What Else Is Different?

Traders are often attracted to weekly options because a relatively small investment is required. If I have a $5,000 account, I can easily place a couple of trades every week and quickly build my account size. But that knife cuts both ways – I could lose half of my account in less than a week!

Another attraction to weekly options is simply the "action", i.e., the result of my trade is known rather quickly and then I can place a new trade. Some options strategies rely on time decay of options over a longer period of time, perhaps 60 days or more. Some traders regard this as tantamount to "watching paint dry" and thus much prefer the faster pace of weekly options strategies. As in other aspects of trading, one must match up the trader's comfort with risk and his trading style with the characteristics of the particular trading strategy.

Traders often ignore the cost of trading commissions. Perform this experiment:

1. Estimate the amount you spent on commissions over the past year.
2. Now go to your broker's web site and run the report to see how much you actually spent.
3. Are you surprised?

Many traders fail to realize that trading weekly options will dramatically increase their commission expenses. If we are using a multi-legged strategy like the iron condor, it will be even more surprising. Commissions are simply a cost of doing business; they aren't good or bad, but I need to minimize those costs. If I know my costs of doing business are rising, I must ensure that my profits are also rising proportionally.

Risk management is the most critical aspect of successful trading. In my opinion, managing the risk of weekly options positions is often overlooked. Some options strategies lend themselves to adjustments and hedging to manage the position over time, thus minimizing losses and salvaging gains when the market moves against us. The short lifetime of weekly options precludes those adjustment and hedging techniques for risk management of these positions. Our weekly option position may move so far against us overnight or over the weekend, that our adjustment would be "too little and too late".

For this reason, our weekly option positions will generally have very simple stop loss rules based on the overall loss of the position or hitting a critical price of the underlying stock. Since we have seen that the values of our weekly options can change by large amounts in relatively short periods of time, our losses are likely to be larger when we stop out a position. This isn't necessarily bad in and of itself, but it does dictate that our gains have to be much larger to be successful over time.

Possible Strategies With Weekly Options

In theory, one could use weekly options in virtually any options strategy. Some traders prefer weekly options for speculative trades based on their prediction of a short-term price move. The advantage of that trade is the reduced investment required. But the disadvantage is the lack of any extra time for the move to occur if our time prediction is off by a few days. Many options traders make it their practice to buy one or two months of extra time in their positions just to give their predictions a little more time to work out as predicted. Traders of weekly options do not have that luxury.

The rapid time decay of weekly options lends itself to strategies that derive their gains based on time decay, i.e., selling options. Possible candidate strategies follow.

1. Iron Condor Spreads With Weekly Options

Iron condor spreads are often used as delta neutral options strategies by traders looking for steady income generation (a detailed discussion of the iron condor strategy is covered in Chapter 13). If we use weekly index options for the iron condor spread, we can easily create a trade with the potential to earn about 15% within a week – that's huge! But the trader's first reaction to that prospect should be to determine the downside risk, because we know there's no free lunch in options trading. Figure 6.1 displays the price chart for the Russell 2000 Index (RUT) and the risk/reward curve for an iron condor created with weekly options with 8 days until expiration.

The two light horizontal lines in Figure 6.1 around $1179 and $1231 represent the break-even prices of the position. If RUT stays within those prices for the next week, this trade has the potential for a 15% return. But how are we going to manage the risk? I would suggest using the 200% rule: monitor the debit to close each spread; when the debit to close one side of the condor is double the original credit received to open that spread, my stop loss has triggered and I close all of the spreads on that side.

You will find that this trade set-up and use of the 200% rule will result in many trades being stopped out early, but this approach should give the trader a better chance at long-term profitability. Other adjustments for the iron condor are discussed in Chapter 13, but there is insufficient time in a weekly option position for those adjustments to be feasible. Trading the iron condor with weekly options is an aggressive trade. The position can easily move near a maximum loss overnight or over a weekend. Longer term options give the trader more time for hedging and adjustments.

Figure 6.1
RUT Iron Condor With Weekly Options
Source: *Screenshots provided courtesy of Optionetics Platinum © 2014. All rights reserved, etc.*

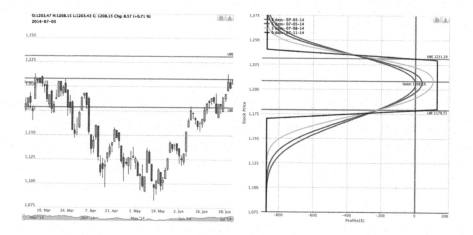

2. Covered Calls With Weekly Options

The covered call options strategy is considered one of the more conservative ways to use options in your stock portfolio. On July 3, 2014, IBM closed at $188.53. We could have sold the Aug $190 call for $2.62. If IBM were trading above $190 at expiration (43 days later), the stock would be called away and the trader would receive a gain of about 2.2% in a little more than a month.

By contrast, if the trader instead sold the July week two $190 call for $0.74 and IBM were trading above $190 at expiration eight days later, the stock would be called away and the trader would receive a 1.2% gain in about a week. And the trader could repeat this trade six more times before the August monthly option expiration. So the profit potential for the covered call using weekly options is enhanced.

This enhanced gain with the covered call is not unprecedented. We would make the same observations if we compared selling a LEAPS call against our stock position versus selling monthly calls throughout the year. Selling premium more frequently always yields the potential of a larger return longer term. Therefore, just as selling ten or twelve monthly calls rather than one LEAPS call brings in a larger return, the same principle holds true for selling our calls on a weekly basis.

One of the advantages enjoyed by the covered call trader is the added downside protection as compared to the stockholder. The premium for the call we received gives us a little room to be comfortable as the stock price pulls back. Traders enter a stop loss for the covered call at or below the break-even price for the trade. In the example above with the monthly option, the price of IBM may drop roughly three or four dollars before our stop loss would be triggered. However, the break-even price with the weekly option is much tighter, less than a dollar. Therein lies the trade-off. With weekly options in our covered call, we will be stopped out more often, or, at a minimum, we will frequently be forced to hold the underwater trade while waiting for the stock price to recover.

3. Diagonal Spreads With Weekly Options

Diagonal bull call spreads are formed by buying an ITM call in a future expiration month and selling the OTM call in the front month. As expiration approaches, we have a decision facing us:

> ➢ If the underlying stock price is trading near or above the strike price we sold, we roll the short call out to the next month by buying back the short call in the front month and selling the same strike in the next expiration month.
> ➢ If the underlying stock price is trading below the strike price we sold, we allow the call to expire worthless and then we sell the OTM call for next month.

If the underlying stock trades up strongly, we will find ourselves rolling our short ITM calls forward for smaller credits and will eventually be forced to close the position, but it often will be closed for a nice gain.

This trading strategy can be deployed precisely the same way, except by selling weekly call options against the longer term monthly or LEAPS call option. Similarly to what we saw with the covered calls, we will find that the returns of the diagonal bull call strategy using weekly calls will be significantly larger than what we experienced when using monthly calls. Again, selling premium more frequently leads to larger returns. But we also will have a tighter lower break-even price, just as we saw with the covered call.

4. Butterfly Spreads With Weekly Options

Butterfly spreads are often used as income generation trades and this trade is discussed in detail in Chapter 11. A butterfly may be established with weekly options exactly as we would with monthly options. We sell two ATM calls and then move one or two strikes higher and buy an OTM call. Then we move downward the same distance and buy one ITM call. We may also build the butterfly with puts or build an iron butterfly with credit spreads on either side (see Chapter 11 for those details).

One difference you will notice with weekly options is that it isn't practical to broaden the butterfly's wings very much; traders often broaden the wings to achieve a wider profitability range. But we will be limited with weekly options as we attempt to broaden the wings. Deep ITM and far OTM options may be listed, but they will usually have zero open interest and the bid/ask spread will be huge. For example, with IBM trading at $196, the weekly $170 call has zero open interest and the bid/ask spread is $4.25 wide. As a practical matter, I would be restricted to the $180 and $210 calls for a weekly butterfly with $15 wings. By contrast, the wings on my monthly butterfly could be $70 wide before I ran into limited open interest.

I can manage the risk of my weekly butterfly by closing the trade if the break-even price on either side is hit, but adjustments won't be feasible because of insufficient time remaining to expiration. Since the wings of my weekly butterfly will be relatively narrow, I will be stopped out of this position frequently. But the attraction is selling two ATM options that are expiring in just a few days, so I can generate a quick profit if the stock or index price cooperates. The rapid time decay of the weekly option is driving the profitability of the weekly butterfly.

What Can Go Wrong?

At this point the reader might reasonably think, "This sounds too good. What can go wrong?" The answer lies within the factor that causes weekly options to be attractive in the first place: large financial leverage over a short period of time. Weekly options offer the trader the opportunity to extract large gains from the market in a matter of only a few days. However, that leverage works both ways.

When stock traders begin to trade options, they are often surprised by the enhanced role of time in their success. If the trader is bullish on Google, buys 100 shares of stock, and then Google trades sideways for thirty days, that probably doesn't cause much concern. But when the options trader is bullish on Google and buys a call option, she realizes the clock is ticking. The options trader does not have the luxury of waiting for her prediction to be proven correct. The criticality of the trader's time prediction is magnified with weekly options. Our weekly option position may dramatically gain or lose value overnight or over a weekend.

Minor stock price moves will be magnified in our weekly option position and that may translate to large gains or large losses in a matter of hours. Strict discipline to stop out losing positions and to close positions early for a profit will serve the trader of weekly options well. As in all options trading, risk management of the weekly options strategy will make the critical difference between long-term gains or losses.

The primary focus of this book is non-directional trading. Some of my students like to trade non-directionally with weekly options. However, I generally discourage the practice. When the trader doesn't have any alternatives for adjusting or hedging the position, non-directional trading is very difficult. In my personal accounts, I sell weekly calls against my stock or long call positions, and I use weekly options to play earnings announcements. But I use monthly options for my non-directional trading.

Summary

The availability of weekly options is relatively recent, but weekly options for the broad market indexes and individual stocks have been growing rapidly in popularity. New weekly options for stocks are being added every month. The exercise and settlement characteristics of weekly options often parallel their monthly option cousins, but critical exceptions exist. Be sure you know the specifications for the weekly options you are trading in advance of placing the trade.

The profit and loss of weekly options positions can move rapidly, often overnight. This makes the role of risk management particularly challenging and critical to long-term success. Weekly options offer the potential for more frequent trading, and therefore, larger gains over the long term. However, one must always monitor trading commissions to be sure the increased trading costs do not overwhelm one's gains.

Many options strategies may be used with weekly options; the rapid time decay of weekly options suggests the trader focus on selling option premium; iron condors, butterflies, covered calls, and diagonal bull call spreads are examples of these strategies. The rapid moves that frequently occur in weekly option values underscore the criticality of the risk management required for these trades. However, many of the possible adjustments we normally would utilize are not available when trading weekly options – there simply isn't enough time. So trade management will be more challenging. These characteristics present a significant disadvantage to the non-directional trader.

Weekly options offer the trader new opportunities for trading every week, but the positions need to be managed carefully. These are not positions that may be established and then forgotten. Risk management is even more critical with the increased leverage of weekly options.

CHAPTER SEVEN

THE UBIQUITOUS VERTICAL SPREAD

Option spreads are created when we buy one option and simultaneously sell another option. When the two options are within the same expiration month, the spread is known as a vertical spread. The vertical spread derives its name from the early days of options trading when the prices were posted in the exchange with the strike prices listed vertically and the different expiration months listed horizontally across the top. Spreads that were created by buying and selling options within the same expiration month were called vertical spreads since both options were in the same vertical column.

Vertical spreads are always directional trades. The trader has predicted a price for the underlying stock or index and a time period for the price move to occur. The vertical spread profits if the trader's prediction proves correct. But the focus of this book is non-directional trading, i.e., avoiding the need to predict the future price of the underlying stock or index. A thorough understanding of the vertical spread is important foundational knowledge for the non-directional trader because vertical spreads are the building blocks of the some of the more complex non-directional trading strategies we discuss in detail in future chapters.

Building the Vertical Spread

Let's revisit a vertical spread example from Chapter 5, but we will develop the example in more detail here. With Qualcomm (QCOM) trading at $81 on July 8th, 2014, I could have bought a QCOM Aug $80 call for $2.41 or $241 for one contract. I could have then created a spread by selling the QCOM Aug $85 call for $0.53 or $53. I created the QCOM Aug 80/85 call spread for $188. If QCOM closes at expiration above $85 per share, then the person who bought the $85 call option will exercise that call, requiring me to sell 100 shares of QCOM stock at $85 per share. But I will exercise my $80 call and buy 100 shares of QCOM at $80 per share and then use those shares to satisfy the $85 call exercised against me. So I bought QCOM at $80 and sold it at $85, and that leaves me with $500 in my account. I spent $188 establishing the trade so my net profit is $312 or 166%.

This vertical spread is often called a bull call spread, since it is built with calls and would be used when you have a bullish expectation for a stock. We may also have created a bullish vertical put spread on QCOM by buying the $80 put for $1.69 and selling the $85 put for $4.82. In this case, we received more for the option we sold than the option we purchased, so we had a net cash flow into our account, or a credit of $313. For this spread, the maximum profit is attained when QCOM closes above $85 at expiration and both put options expire worthless. The original credit of $313 would then be the profit. This vertical put spread is often called a bull put spread.

When the option we sold is priced higher than the option we bought, we have created a credit spread. When the option we bought is more costly than the option we sold, we have a net cash flow out of our account, or a debit; we have created a debit spread. Often traders will say they have "bought a call spread", meaning they built a debit spread with calls. The above QCOM example with puts would be called "selling a put spread" or establishing a bull put spread. This terminology is summarized below.

Table 7.1
Vertical Spread Terminology

Calls or Puts in Spread	Posture	Retail Name	Pit Name	Credit or Debit
Calls	Bullish	Bull Call Spread	Buying a Call Spread	Debit
Calls	Bearish	Bear Call Spread	Selling a Call Spread	Credit
Puts	Bullish	Bull Put Spread	Selling a Put Spread	Credit
Puts	Bearish	Bear Put Spread	Buying a Put Spread	Debit

Let's return to our first example of the QCOM Aug 80/85 bull call spread. This spread could be established for a debit of $188 for one contract. The maximum loss for any debit spread is simply the original debit. The maximum profit for any debit spread is found by subtracting the debit from the value of the spread; if the two strike prices of the spread are $10 apart, the spread value is $1,000; if $5 apart, then the value is $500 and so on. For this example, the maximum profit is $312 (500 − 188) and the return is 166% (profit divided by the capital at risk or 312/188).

The QCOM Aug 80/85 bull put spread could be established for a credit of $313 so the maximum potential profit is the credit or $313 and the maximum potential loss is the spread less the credit or $187. The potential return is 167%.

Notice that the debit call spread has essentially the same return as the credit spread at the same strike prices, so there is no inherent advantage to using the debit spread or the credit spread to profit from the trader's bullish prediction. The choice of a credit or a debit spread is principally one of style preference. Some prefer a credit spread because they can earn interest on the credit monies in their accounts while in the trade; but this presumes larger numbers of contracts and that interest rates are higher than we have experienced in recent years. Another advantage of credit spreads is fewer trading commissions, assuming the spread is allowed to expire worthless. The profit and loss calculations for vertical spreads are summarized in Table 7.2.

Table 7.2
Vertical Spread Return Calculations

Debit or Credit Spread	Maximum Profit	Maximum Loss	% Return
Debit	Spread - Debit	Debit	[(Spread − Debit) /Debit] x 100
Credit	Credit	Spread - Credit	[Credit/(Spread − Credit)] x 100

Effects of Implied Volatility

One of the commonly repeated myths associated with options trading is:

When implied volatility is high, sell credit spreads, and when implied volatility is low, buy debit spreads.

In this section we will show why that statement isn't true, but don't jump to the conclusion that implied volatility may be ignored.

We saw in our examples with QCOM in the previous section that the returns of the bullish credit spread and the bullish debit spread, placed at the same strike prices, were virtually identical. Consider two more examples from July 7th, 2014. Dish Networks (DISH) was trading at $66 and its ATM implied volatility was relatively high at 47%. This level of volatility was in the 98th percentile of implied volatility history for DISH. The percentile level tells us that the implied volatility level of DISH has only been higher 2% of the time in the past two years. The August 60/65 bull call spread would have cost $325 and would have returned 54% if DISH closed over $65 at August expiration. However, when we looked at the Aug 60/65 bull put spread, we found it would have brought in a credit of $173 and therefore could have returned 53% if successful. Thus, the credit and debit spreads at the same strikes for a high implied volatility stock had virtually identical returns. If the myth were true, the credit spread should have had an advantage with this high volatility stock.

Consider a low implied volatility example on the same day. Autozone (AZO) was trading at $538 with an ATM implied volatility of 14%, which ranked in the first percentile of recent history. The August 540/550 bull call spread would have cost $395 to establish and would have returned a maximum of 153%. If the myth were true, this debit spread should have the superior return, but the August 540/550 bull put spread would have brought in a credit of $610 and therefore had a maximum potential return of 156%. Again, we see the same result. The credit and debit spreads at the same strike prices for a low implied volatility stock had virtually identical returns.

This example teaches us two important lessons:

1. The returns from the debit spread and the credit spread at the same strikes will always be equivalent.
2. A vertical spread is the option investment trade of choice in a high volatility environment when buying the individual option would be very expensive.

This second point bears some emphasis. If the trader is bullish on a stock, the simplest trade is to buy a call option. But if implied volatility is very high, that call option will be expensive. That long call option position carries risk from not only the stock price declining, but also from a decline in implied volatility. Of course, an alternative for that situation would be to sell a put option; now the trader is benefiting from the bullish prediction, but also benefiting from the high level of implied volatility. But the naked short option (call or put) carries a large downside risk. Using a contingent stop loss order may limit some of that risk, but buying a long put below that short put option limits the trader's risk to a specific maximum amount. The vertical spread is an excellent choice for the high volatility environment when buying an expensive option would require a large investment and selling an option is accompanied by large downside risk.

So the trader may be indifferent to the choice of the debit spread or the credit spread when volatility is extremely high or low. But what happens if implied volatility shifts while we are in the vertical spread?

First of all, recall how the spread makes its profit. When we establish a ten-dollar wide credit spread and the options expire worthless, we simply keep the credit we received initially – no more and no less. Similarly, both options of the debit spread will expire in the money so they will both be exercised, leaving the value of the spread, or $1,000 in the account (for a ten-dollar spread). The difference between the original debit and the spread value is the maximum profit. High or low implied volatility can't change these facts. But changes in implied volatility do affect the value of our spread throughout the time period before expiration.

Figure 7.1 shows the risk/reward graph for a Google (GOOGL) 575/585 bull call spread on July 7th, 2014 with Google at $582. For one contract, the initial debit was $535 and the maximum gain was $465.

This graphic comes from Platinum, an options analysis software package. On the left of Figure 7.1 is a standard candlestick price chart for Google. On the right is the risk/reward diagram for this option spread. The heavy black line is the value of the position at expiration as a function of varying prices of Google. Take your pencil from any price on the price chart and draw horizontally across to the risk/reward chart to see the profit or loss at expiration. I personally like this presentation of the risk/reward chart because I can easily see the profit or loss of the option position corresponding to the various support and resistance levels on the price chart.

The value of the spread varies with time to expiration, implied volatility, and the price of the underlying stock. Interest rates and dividends will also affect spread values, but these will be less significant effects. The effects of time decay are shown by the colored lines in the risk/reward chart on the right hand side of the chart from Platinum. The red line shows the value of the spread today at various prices of the underlying stock or index, GOOGL in this case. The remaining time until expiration of the options in this spread is divided into thirds. The blue line displays the value of the spread after one third of the time until expiration has elapsed, and the green line shows the value at two thirds of the time until expiration. And finally, the black line shows the profit or loss at various prices of Google at expiration.

These time decay curves show quantitatively what spread traders observe every day, i.e., the underlying stock price may have moved as predicted above or below the spread strike prices, but the spread cannot be closed for a value close to the maximum theoretical profit until we near expiration. The value of the spread will gradually approach the maximum profit as the time value of the options decays to zero. In Figure 7.1, we see that if our prediction were for Google to trade at $600 at 13 days to expiration, we would expect to be able to close the position for a gain of approximately $250. But if we wait until expiration, the position will gain $465 for any price of Google above $585.

Figure 7.2 shows the risk graph for our Google call spread assuming implied volatility has continually increased over the life of the trade, ending at a value 25% higher at expiration. Increasing implied volatility during the trade results in the time decay curves being flattened toward an imaginary diagonal line drawn between the maximum gain and maximum loss limits of the trade. Imagine the time decay curve for today in Figure 7.1 as a string and we pull it taut. The practical effect for the trader is that the value of the spread approaches the ultimate value at expiration more slowly. Therefore, the probability of closing the trade early for a majority of the maximum profit is reduced.

Figure 7.1
Risk/Reward Graph For a GOOGL Bull Call Spread
Source: *Screenshots provided courtesy of Optionetics Platinum © 2014. All rights reserved, etc.*

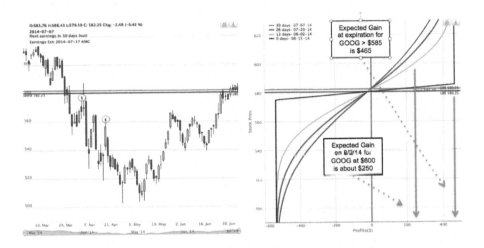

Note how the green line at thirteen days to expiration in Figure 7.2 has pulled away from the curve for the day of expiration (the heavy black line). We could only expect to close the trade early for about $200. The increased level of implied volatility has decreased the gains by about 18%. Therefore, closing the trade with thirteen days to expiration would achieve less of the potential profit if implied volatility has increased during the trade. However, the maximum profit at expiration is unchanged by the increased implied volatility. You just have to remain in the trade until expiration to receive it.

The flattening effect on the time decay curves due to increasing implied volatility during the life of the trade is identical for credit and debit vertical spreads. Therefore, if one is expecting a large implied volatility increase, such as we might see in advance of an earnings announcement, there is no inherent advantage to either a credit or a debit spread. But one should expect to have to carry the trade closer to expiration to achieve a majority of the potential profit if implied volatility increases.

Figure 7.2
GOOGL Bull Call Spread With Increased Implied Volatility
Source: *Screenshots provided courtesy of Optionetics Platinum © 2014. All rights reserved, etc.*

Figure 7.3 displays the risk/reward curves for this same Google 575/585 bull call spread with implied volatility reduced by 25% during the life of the trade. Decreasing implied volatility results in the time decay curves shifting toward the curve at expiration and increases the separation between the individual curves. The practical effect for the trader is that the value of the spread approaches the ultimate value at expiration more quickly. Therefore, the probability of closing the trade early for a majority of the maximum profit has increased. Now we see that we could close the trade with thirteen days to expiration for a gain of about $320 with Google at $600, an increase of about 28%. However, in both cases, the return for Google at $600 at expiration is unchanged at $465.

Figure 7.3
GOOGL Bull Call Spread With Decreased Implied Volatility

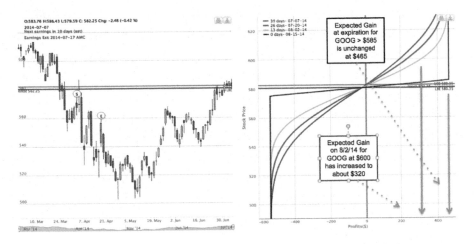

Changes in implied volatility during the time we are in a vertical spread will affect the proportion of the profit available to us if we wish to close the trade early, but it does not affect the ultimate profitability at expiration.

The myth to use credit spreads when implied volatility is high and debit spreads when implied volatility is low may be a confusion that arose out of long and short option positions. It is indeed true that one should consider buying low volatility options and selling high volatility options. If we are considering a long call or put position, we would look for options with low implied volatility because these are inexpensive options. Similarly, we would target high implied volatility options if we were considering selling calls or puts. High volatility options are expensive options, so it seems reasonable to profit from selling those options. But a spread is different. In that case, I am not only selling an expensive option; I am also buying an expensive option.

Therefore, when playing the stock's directional move with a vertical spread strategy, the choice of a credit or debit spread is largely a personal preference. Some prefer a credit spread because they can earn interest on the credit monies in their accounts while in the trade; another advantage of credit spreads is fewer trading commissions (assuming the spread is allowed to expire worthless). Others prefer debit spreads because they have spent the maximum that can be lost on the trade; there is no possibility of an ugly surprise later if the trade turns against them (as there is for a credit spread). But even though that situation may feel different, the ultimate risk/reward situation is identical for the debit spread and the credit spread.

The returns for credit and debit spreads will be identical, and implied volatility levels at the onset of the trade are not a factor in our evaluation of whether to use a credit spread or a debit spread. The effect of the volatility (either high or low) effectively cancels itself out by the opposite nature of the two legs of the spread. Thus, vertical spreads are an excellent way to trade high volatility options when the alternative of establishing a long call or put option position would be much more expensive. But we do pay for that advantage by limiting our maximum gain with the spread.

Early Exercise

All stock options may be exercised on any business day prior to expiration. These are known as American style options. European style options can only be exercised at expiration. Most, but not all, broad index options are European style, e.g., SPX, RUT, NDX, and others. The OEX (S&P 100) is a notable example of an index option with American style exercise. Be sure to check the option exchange web site for the specifications of exercise for the options you are trading – don't be surprised!

When you have bought or sold stock option vertical spreads, early exercise of one or more of the options in your spreads is always a possibility, but actually only occurs under very specific circumstances. The owner of an equity option has the right to buy or sell 100 shares of the underlying stock any time before expiration. If you are long the option, i.e., you originally bought it, you may or may not choose to exercise the option you own; it is entirely your choice. If you are short the option, i.e., you originally sold the option, it may be exercised against you at any time. Typically, you will receive an email from your broker after the market closes, notifying you of the exercise. You may be exercised for only a portion of your option position, e.g., only 2 of your 10 contracts, or you may be exercised for your entire position. If you were short call options, you will now see a short stock position in your account, i.e., you were obligated to sell the stock at the strike price. If you were short put options, the exercise forces you to buy stock at the strike price, resulting in a long stock position in your account.

Early exercise with vertical spreads is normally not anything to be concerned about. If we owned ten contracts of an IBM call spread and three of our short calls are exercised against us, we would then be short 300 shares of IBM, i.e., we sold 300 shares of IBM to satisfy the exercise. We could then ask our broker to exercise three of our long IBM calls and buy 300 shares of stock. Now the short position in IBM is eliminated and we have seven remaining call spreads and the spread difference in cash in our account, i.e., $3,000 if a ten dollar spread. In practice, you will usually find that the broker will automatically satisfy the exercise of your short options by exercising the long options in the spread. Check with your broker to confirm his policies.

In my experience, it is rare that your short option positions in a vertical spread will be exercised against you before expiration. But, as noted above, your long option position protects you against this exercise. In general, put options are rarely exercised unless there is less than $0.10 of time value left in the option. The same is true of call options with one major exception. Calls are often exercised just before a stock goes ex-dividend, e.g., if the call has $0.10 of time value remaining, and the dividend is $0.50 per share, then it would be advantageous to the option owner to exercise the option and hold the stock through the ex-dividend date to collect the dividend payment. The trader loses the time value remaining in the option, but gains the larger dividend payment. Sometimes an option will be exercised against you in a situation where it makes no sense whatsoever and is probably a mistake or due to the inexperience of the person on the other side of the trade. But that is of no consequence to the vertical spread – you are protected.

Expiration and Exercise

Upon expiration, your broker will automatically exercise any expiring options in your account that are $0.01 or more ITM (in the money) in accordance with Options Clearing Corporation regulations. If expiration is approaching and the stock price is near your strike price, and you do not want to hold either the long or short stock position that will result from the exercise of your long option, sell the option before the market closes on the Friday of expiration week. European style index options are often settled via morning settlement (AM settlement). The settlement price for these options is determined during the day on the Friday of expiration week and these options cannot be traded after the close of trading on Thursday of expiration week. If you wish to close that position before expiration, be sure to complete those orders before the market closes on the Thursday before expiration. If you wish to exercise any of your long equity options, you may issue an order to your broker at any time before expiration. But if your long equity option is ITM and you allow it to enter expiration, it will be exercised on your behalf. It is generally good practice to close option positions before expiration to avoid unpleasant surprises.

If you are holding a vertical spread position going into expiration, several situations are possible. If both of the options are fully in the money, your broker will automatically exercise both of the long and short options and credit your account with the spread amount less commissions. However, if the stock price closes on expiration Friday within the spread, the situation is a little tricky and the results may surprise you.

Consider the situation where we are holding ten contracts of a bull call spread at the strike prices $100 and $110, and the stock closes at $109 on expiration Friday. The short $110 calls will expire worthless and the broker will exercise the $100 calls on your behalf, resulting in 1000 shares of stock in your account the following Monday (and perhaps a call from your broker if your account does not have sufficient cash to buy the stock). If you do not want to purchase the stock, you should close the spread before the market closes on the Friday of expiration week.

Another example results in a short stock position. If I have sold ten contracts of the 170/180 bear call spread and the underlying stock closes on the Friday of expiration week at $178, my short $170 call options will be exercised against me, resulting in my selling 1000 shares of the stock. The long call options do not protect me because they expired worthless. Now I have a large short position in my account and may not have sufficient cash and margin to cover that position. In most cases, your broker will close the spread Friday afternoon to limit the firm's exposure.

If the stock price closes on expiration Friday within the strike prices of my vertical spread, it will result in either a long stock position or a short stock position in my account the following Monday. Unless you are willing to hold that stock position, it is usually best to close the spread on Friday. Many traders adopt a rule of closing all option positions the week before expiration to avoid the surprises that are all too common during the week of expiration.

Margin Requirements

When opening a stock trading account, one always has the option of establishing a cash account or a margin account. If you have a margin account, you have the ability to buy more shares of a stock by borrowing additional funds from the brokerage firm. This is known as buying on margin and can lead to *margin calls* if the stock price declines. The margin call will require the deposit of additional funds or the sale of the stock position. Each month's statement will include interest charged by the broker for the margin.

We also speak of margin requirements in options trading accounts, but the concept is completely different; no borrowing is involved. When you establish an options position in your account, the broker determines the worst case scenario and sets aside a *margin requirement* in your account and does not allow you to establish any new positions with those funds. The money is still in your account and earns interest, but can be thought of as being placed in escrow. This insures the broker in the event the position takes its maximum potential loss. The broker wants to be sure you can't lose more money than on deposit in the account because the brokerage would be exposed to that loss if you catch the plane to Acapulco.

For example, I establish an 80/90 bull put spread for a $2,000 credit on 10 contracts. The cash balance in my account increases by $2,000, but the broker sets aside $10,000 as a margin requirement, including the $2,000 credit. In the worst case scenario, the maximum loss for that ten contract spread would be $10,000, hence the margin requirement of

$10,000. I will be unable to use this $10,000 for any other trades until this credit spread is closed.

Selection Of Strike Prices

The risk and reward characteristics of vertical spreads vary dramatically depending on the positioning of the spread, or the choice of the strike prices for the spread. Traders generally categorize vertical spreads as ITM (in the money), ATM (at the money) or OTM (out of the money). In Table 7.3, we illustrate this concept with several spreads for IBM on 7/9/14 with IBM trading at $188, using the August options.

Table 7.3
Selected IBM Bull Call Spreads

Spread	Debit	Max gain	Return	Probability
170/180	$893	$107	12%	75%
180/190	$618	$392	62%	43%
190/200	$250	$750	300%	17%

In each case, we have calculated the probability of the stock price closing above the spread at expiration. The ITM spread at 170/180 will cost the most to establish at $893, has the smallest return at 12%, but also has the highest probability of success at 75%. This is the calculated probability of IBM closing at a price above $180 at August expiration. As we position our spread more ATM and then OTM, we see that the probability of success is dropping significantly, but our cost to establish the spread is much lower and the returns are much higher. This is one of the most basic rules of finance; higher rewards are always accompanied by higher risk.

Traders often focus on the risk/reward ratio of the trade under consideration, where the risk is the maximum loss and the reward is the maximum gain. For the IBM bull call spreads of Table 7.3, the debit to establish the spread is the maximum loss and the maximum gain is simply the difference between the ten-dollar spread, or $1,000, and the debit. So the risk/reward ratio is largest for the deep ITM spread and smallest for the OTM spread.

A myth of option trading is to insist on trades where the maximum profit is two or three times as large as the maximum loss. These are trades with small risk/reward ratios and they have low probabilities of success. Often beginning traders are taught to place these "low risk" trades, but are not told that they are placing a trade with a low probability of profit.

Option traders have conventionally referred to the ITM spread as the high probability trade, or the conservative trade, and the OTM spread as the aggressive or risky trade. But note that while the conservative trade has the highest probability of success, it also has the largest maximum loss. There is a low probability of that loss, but if the loss occurs, it will be large. Conservative traders are often misled by the high probability of success and equate this trade with a conservative investment, such as treasury bills. This conservative options spread is similar in that the probability of success is high and the gain is relatively small compared to other option spreads. But the maximum loss is quite large. It has a low probability of occurrence, but it will be painful if it occurs.

These principles are typical of all options strategies. If the trade I am considering has a high probability of success, I know that this trade inherently has a large potential loss. Risk management is always a crucial aspect of trading, but it is especially important for the high probability trade.

There isn't a right or wrong trade for IBM in Table 7.3; each of these spreads is a feasible trade candidate. But it is crucial to understand the trade-offs in risk and reward as well as the probabilities of success for these positions. Match the trade to your price and time predictions, your personal style, and your risk tolerance.

Summary

Vertical spreads are perhaps the most commonly used options strategy; these are directional trades and therefore are not the focus of this book. However, vertical spreads are the building blocks of the non-directional trading strategies, such as the butterfly and condor spreads. Those strategies are the focus of this book, so understanding the vertical spread is important foundational knowledge for the non-directional trader.

Vertical spreads may be formed as credit or debit spreads; the debit spread and the credit spread created at the same strike prices will always have virtually the same maximum gain and maximum loss. The preferences between the debit and credit spread are largely derived from the trader's personal style.

Implied volatility is not a factor when establishing the vertical spread; in fact, the vertical spread is an excellent alternative to a long option position in times of high volatility. Implied volatility may shift while in the trade, but this does not affect the ultimate profitability of the spread. However, an increase in implied volatility while in the spread will make it difficult to close the trade early; the profitable position will be closed for a smaller gain than expected and the losing position will be closed for a larger loss than expected. Decreasing implied volatility would have the opposite effect, making it more feasible to close the trade early for a large proportion of the gain, or a smaller loss.

The vertical spread may be positioned in the money (ITM), at the money (ATM) or out of the money (OTM). As we move from ITM to OTM, the risk/reward ratio will decrease, and the maximum gains will increase, but the probability of success is decreasing. All of these vertical spreads are feasible, but the trader must position the spread in accordance with her price and time predictions, her personal trading style, and her risk tolerance.

The vertical spread is a powerful and versatile tool that may be used in a variety of situations to profit from one's predictions for a stock's price movement. Vertical spreads may also be combined to form more complicated options trading strategies. A solid understanding of the vertical spread will prove very helpful for the options trader. The vertical spread is indeed ubiquitous.

CHAPTER EIGHT

DOES YOUR HEAD GET IN THE WAY?

The role of the trader's own emotions and psychology is often overlooked in books on the subject of trading, but this subject is crucial to the trader's success. In many ways, it is an extension of the perennial advice to "know yourself". Most of our training as traders occurs the hard way – we learn from our mistakes. And a large part of that process is learning about ourselves and avoiding self-destruction.

The Two Deadly Emotions

Books and articles on the psychology of trading often start with a discussion of fear, but I have found that greed is often even more destructive. We vividly remember that day when the market was crashing and we were watching our hard earned capital vanish before our eyes. We may have been frozen before the monitor, unsure whether to close the position and take the loss, or rely on hope that somehow this move will reverse shortly. We felt that bone chilling fear and its paralyzing effect. And that paralysis normally just leads to a larger loss.

However, we may not recall the losing trade we established after a string of huge winners. We were euphoric. That euphoria led to our beginning to ignore our own trading rules and gradually we began taking more and more risk. We were privately convinced that we had this game all figured out. Just as fear led us astray and caused us to "freeze in the headlights", greed can inflate our ego and cause just as much damage in our trading account.

Developing an unemotional, systematic approach to your trading and investments is crucial for success. The first step is developing your trading system. Throughout this book, I emphasize the use of a set of trading and risk management rules for every trading strategy. That is your trading system. Notice that I said this is "your" trading system. Don't be deceived into thinking someone out there has the "silver bullet", or the best trading system. To be sure, a trading mentor or coach will be very helpful as you develop the foundation of knowledge for trading options and then begin live trading. But the ultimate responsibility for developing a trading system suited to your style and risk tolerance is yours alone. You will find that much of the value of the trading coach is his or her advice while you are in the midst of trading. You will likely find yourself very anxious about a particular trade and the calm perspective and analysis of your trading coach will be invaluable.

I was recently discussing my private coaching services with a prospective client. He told me he had lost over ten thousand dollars in the previous six months trading options. After a lengthy discussion, he told me he thought spending two thousand dollars on my coaching was just too much money to spend on his trading education – I found that fascinating. Somehow, he thought losing ten thousand dollars trading was acceptable, but investing a much smaller amount in his own education was a waste of money.

The right trading coach will learn about your trading style and risk profile, and help you develop the trading system that fits you. Trading systems help us structure our thinking and our trading. But the most important function of a trading system is as a tool to help us control our emotions.

Our objective is to minimize the effects of emotions in our trading. We will never fully eliminate emotion from our trading, and judgment will always be an important ingredient in our success. The trading system is designed to systematize our trading, minimize the destructive effect of our emotions, and minimize our risk exposure.

How Did You Succeed In Life?

Options traders all share a very important characteristic. They have all been successful in some profession before discovering option trading. The stark reality is that one has to have developed a reasonable amount of capital in order to make option trading a viable alternative. Many unscrupulous promoters will sell their trading systems with the idea that one can start with a few hundred dollars and turn that into a million dollars in short order. The customers that bite on that infomercial will be out of business quickly.

Are you a perfectionist? In my experience, many, if not all, of my coaching students are perfectionists – that characteristic was fundamental to their success. That characteristic may have served them well in their professional careers, but it will be a liability as they trade options.

You are successful in your professional capacity because you always deliver first quality products and services. You take the extra effort to make it right – every time. But options trading is a probabilistic business. You will have losses. The key to success is managing the losses so that we have net gains over the long term. That is the role of risk management. The perfectionist finds the reality of those losses hard to accept. They have trained themselves through their own experience that success comes from hard work and preparation – and it isn't a matter of being successful 60 or 70% of the time. That win/loss ratio would have led to failure in their professions, but it can easily lead to long-term profits in options trading.

I emphasize risk management throughout this book and we discussed more detailed aspects of risk management and money management in Chapter 3. But the successful application of risk management techniques does not mean my account will never have a loss. Losses are a natural and expected result of trading. In my trading business, losses are simply one of the costs of doing business, like trading commissions. Monitoring and minimizing business expenses is a crucial part of any business. Accepting those losses as a normal aspect of the trading business is difficult for the perfectionist.

A common pitfall for the perfectionist is to change the rules in his trading system after every loss he experiences. Effectively, he no longer has a trading system. The unexamined premise in his thinking is that he should be able to correctly analyze the trade and always be profitable. He is searching for the perfect trading system. That is an unrealistic expectation.

The Two-Headed Monster

We are focusing on non-directional trading strategies in this book. But I expect the reader is not much different than I am. I have several different investment accounts; some are focused on my retirement; some have the goal of educating my grandchildren. I trade most of these accounts directionally, but I also trade non-directionally for income. When trading your prediction for the move of a stock or index price, you have many technical and fundamental analysis tools at your disposal. But trading non-directionally is completely different – a prediction of market price or direction isn't required. In fact, managing my position on the basis of my market prediction may actually get me into trouble. For example, I open my iron condor position according to my trading system rules. My trigger to adjust the position is tripped, but I choose not to adjust my position because my technical indicators have convinced me that the market is going to pull back. I started out trading non-directionally, but I have now poisoned my trading system with a directional bias. That is the danger of the Two-Headed Monster. We are of two minds: one has established trading rules for a non-directional trade, but the other is predicting the future.

One can't run a trading business without an interest in the market and the variety of forces underlying its moves. When we add to that the management of the directional trades in other accounts, we introduce the risk of our directional bias polluting our non-directional trading system. One of my heads is managing my directional trades; I am drawing support and resistance levels, predicting a move after the upcoming FOMC announcement, watching trading volume, moving averages, Bollinger Bands, MACD, and perhaps several other indicators. This part of my mind is trying its best to make sense out of the myriad information available and predict the future. But I am also monitoring my non-directional position, referring back to my trading system rules, and deciding what actions, if any, are required based only upon the market price at this moment and my rules.

Success in trading requires both of these viewpoints to be active. For one thing, it would be unusual for a non-directional trader to never have any directional trades ongoing. But I would also argue that the non-directional trader might be well advised to shade some of his rules from time to time based on his market assessment. This may be as simple as establishing the iron condor with a little more safety margin to the downside, so we initiate the trade with the put spreads positioned one strike lower. Another example would be a non-directional trader establishing his ATM iron butterfly and buying an extra long put because he sees VIX is increasing and fears the market may be on the verge of a correction.

So learn to live with the Two-Headed Monster and benefit from directional insights and predictions when appropriate, but don't poison your non-directional trading system by using those predictions to overrule your non-directional trading rules. When I find myself predicting whether this month will be a good month for my non-directional trade, I am no longer trading non-directionally.

Summary

The trader's psychology is a critical factor in his success, regardless of what markets or trading derivatives are in play. The novice trader often assumes that fear is the emotional or psychological problem for the trader. While that is true, the euphoria that follows a string of successful trades may also be detrimental to future trades.

Successful traders develop sets of rules that determine the entry, adjustment, and exits for the trade. We refer to this set of rules as the trading system. The primary purpose of the trading system is to control and minimize our emotions in trading. An important role for a subset of the trading system rules is controlling and managing risk. The trading system is the fundamental tool of the non-directional trader.

Focusing on the rules of the trading system helps the non-directional trader minimize the detrimental effects of emotions in his trading. The non-directional trader must also guard against mixing directional predictions into his non-directional trading. The non-directional trader diligently trades only what the market gives him today, not his prediction for tomorrow.

CHAPTER NINE

CALENDAR SPREADS

Calendar spreads are created by buying an option in a future expiration month and selling an option at the same strike price in the current or front expiration month. Calendar spreads are also known as time spreads or horizontal spreads. The horizontal spread terminology derives from the original boards in the exchange used to post option prices. Option prices were posted with the strike prices listed vertically and the expiration months displayed horizontally. When we create the calendar spread, we are buying and selling options in the same row (same strike price) but in different columns (different expiration months), hence, the horizontal spread terminology.

The remaining time before the option expires is one of the critical factors determining an option's price. As the price drops due to less time remaining to expiration, we refer to this phenomenon as time decay. But that time decay is not a linear function; it accelerates as the date of expiration approaches. The profitability of the calendar spread is built upon the differential in time decay between the front month option and the longer-term option. We have sold the front month option and it is decaying in price faster than the longer-term option which we own.

We will create a calendar spread with the Standard and Poors 500 Index (SPX) to illustrate the basic characteristics of this spread. On July 22nd, 2014, SPX was trading at $1985 and we bought the SPX September $1985 call and sold the SPX August $1985 call. This created a $1985 Aug/Sep call calendar spread for a net debit of $1,355. The risk/reward graph is illustrated in Figure 9.1.

Figure 9.1
SPX Nov/Dec $1985 Call Calendar Spread

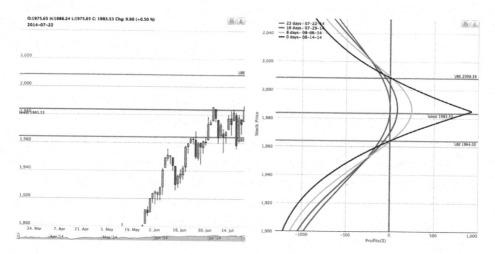

You can immediately see why the calendar spread is attractive with its broad break-even range from $1964 to $2008. This trade has a potential profit of 20% or more over a large portion of that break-even range. This calendar spread was created with call options, but one can also create a calendar using put options. The call calendar and the put calendar at the same strike prices will have similar initial debits and will have virtually identical risk/reward graphs.

These examples of the calendar spread were placed at a strike price near the current stock price. This is the classic *at the money* (ATM) calendar spread. It is used in two similar, but distinct situations:

➤ The trader predicts that the underlying stock or index will trade sideways within a reasonably narrow range (a directional trade).

➤ The non-directional trader may use the ATM calendar spread as an income generation trade and has made no prediction whatsoever.

The directional trader will profit if his prediction for a sideways trading pattern proves correct; the ATM calendar spread will be a profitable trade.

The non-directional trader may use this trade with options on stocks, exchange traded funds (ETFs) or indexes. When broad market index options are used with the ATM calendar spread, a significant advantage is the lack of single stock risk, i.e., the CFO of the company resigns unexpectedly, a major brokerage downgrades the stock, etc. For these reasons, most non-directional traders use ATM calendar spreads on broad market indexes, e.g., the Standard and Poors 500 Index (SPX), the NASDAQ 100 Index (NDX) and the Russell 2000 Index (RUT). Another possibility is to create the calendar spread with the corresponding ETFs for these indexes: SPY, QQQ, and IWM, respectively.

Vega Risk

In Chapter 5 we discussed implied volatility and raised the issue of vega risk, the risk of our trade losing value due to changes in implied volatility. The position vega determines the risk sensitivity to volatility changes. Calendar spreads and double calendar spreads have large positive values of vega and therefore are sensitive to decreases in implied volatility. As an example, let's assume we spent $1,355 to buy one contract of the SPX Aug/Sep $1895 call calendar spread we saw in Figure 9.1. The position Greeks are delta = +$1, vega = +$117, and theta = +$13. The Greeks tell us where our risks are with this trade. If all variables affecting this trade are hypothetically held constant and SPX traded up by $5 to $1418, the delta of +$1 tells us our position value will increase by approximately $5 or less than four tenths of a percent of our investment. If SPX moved down by $5, the position would lose $5, again a very small percentage of our investment. Thus, we call this a delta neutral trade, meaning the position is relatively insensitive to the underlying stock's price movement.

Now consider the passage of time, or what we often call theta decay or time decay. The theta value of +$13 tells us the position will gain $13 in value with the passage of one day; again, this is a relatively small number.

However, as this trade progresses, theta will grow in value and the position will benefit more and more from the passage of time. Time decay is what drives the profitability of the calendar spread. The passage of time is our friend with this trade.

However, our vega value for this position is +$117. An increase of only two percentage points in implied volatility will increase the value of our position by $234 or about 17%. Conversely, a decrease of two points in implied volatility will cause our position to lose 17% of its value. So our position has more sensitivity to changes in implied volatility than anything else. Therefore, we refer to calendar spreads as positions with high vega risk. When we are considering candidates for a calendar spread, it is critical that we compare the current level of implied volatility with the history of implied volatility for this stock or index. Decreasing implied volatility while in a calendar spread will destroy the trade's profitability even if the stock price has stayed exactly where we predicted for the trade's optimum outcome.

We can lose money on calendar spreads principally in two ways: 1) a large price move by the underlying stock or index in either direction, or 2) a decrease in implied volatility. Of these two risks, the vega risk is greater. In my experience, volatility moves have always cost me more on my calendar spreads that went badly.

If we are considering an ATM calendar spread on XYZ stock and we look up the implied volatility of its ATM options, and find it is currently 35%, that may or may not be high. It depends on the stock. However, if we look at the history of implied volatility for this stock and see that it has oscillated over the past year between 25% and 110%, we might feel more confident about this trade. It is more likely that the implied volatility for XYZ will move upward rather than downward, based on its historical pattern of movement and the fact that the current value of implied volatility is near the lower edge of the historical range.

A common pattern of implied volatility movement for most stocks is to peak just before the quarterly earnings announcement and then immediately collapse to historically low values. In Google's early years after its initial public offering (IPO), implied volatility would commonly run up to well over 100% just before its earnings announcement, drop down to about 25%, and then slowly build back to high values before the next earnings announcement. If a company is expecting a significant news event, such as an FDA announcement for a biotechnology company, we will see implied volatility peak just before that announcement.

Aggressive traders may use a calendar spread to benefit from the rise in implied volatility prior to the earnings announcement. But it is crucial that the position is closed prior to the date of the earnings announcement. The collapse in implied volatility after the announcement will destroy the profitability of the calendar spread.

The large vega risk of calendar spreads underscores two critical operational lessons for the calendar spread trader:

1. Ensure the current implied volatility of the stock or index under consideration is in the lower quartile of this stock or index's history of implied volatility.
2. Monitor implied volatility of each leg of the calendar spread during the progress of the trade. Close the position if implied volatility begins to decrease in both legs or if a positive volatility skew begins to develop, i.e., the implied volatility of the front month option is increasing while the back month option's implied volatility is flat or declining.

The discussion thus far has assumed that the two options in our calendar spread have similar or identical values of implied volatility, and that they move together over time. They may have similar values of implied volatility and often move in concert, but one or both of these observations are often not true, and this introduces the concept of the volatility skew.

Volatility Skews

In theory, one might expect a stock's option chain to have similar values of implied volatility across the chain. And that does prove to be a reasonable approximation, but a phenomenon, known as the *volatility smile*, has been observed in broad index options and equity options since the market crash of 1987. The implied volatility of the ITM options and the OTM options tend to have higher values of implied volatility than the ATM options.

The volatility smile is not well understood. Some analysts reason that the higher price of OTM puts may be derived from higher demand for those puts for portfolio protection and the principle of call and put parity then drives higher prices for the corresponding ITM calls. Other analysts start from the position that the higher prices for the ITM calls derive from higher demand for those options as stock surrogates. And then call and put parity drives the corresponding puts higher in price. But either way, you end up in the same place: the values of implied volatility for the OTM puts and the ITM calls tend to be somewhat higher and this constitutes the volatility smile. Occasionally you will see authors refer to the *volatility smirk*, when the two sides of the curve aren't symmetrical.

Similarly, one might expect the implied volatility of two options at the same strike price, but in different expiration months, to be very similar, if not identical. As it turns out, that isn't always true. We have also presumed that implied volatility changes for a stock occur uniformly across the options chain, but that also isn't always true in the real world. Volatility skews in calendar spreads refer to situations where the implied volatility of the front month option that we sold is different from the implied volatility of the option that we purchased in a later month.

A positive volatility skew develops when the implied volatility of the front month is higher than the later month. Conversely, a calendar spread with a negative implied volatility skew has long options in the later month with higher implied volatility than the options that were sold in the front month. Recall what we learned about option pricing in Chapter 5: higher implied volatility means higher option prices. Thus, we would prefer a positive volatility skew where we are selling the more expensive option with higher implied volatility and buying the less expensive option with lower implied volatility, because our profitability is based on the more rapid time decay of the option we sold.

Higher implied volatility develops because the market expects a big move of the stock price, either up or down – it is not a directional prediction. If that higher implied volatility is in the front month, resulting in a positive volatility skew, then the event causing the market's anticipation must be expected in the front month. Similarly, in the case of a negative volatility skew, the market is expecting the catalyst for the big stock price move to occur in the later option expiration month.

An excellent example of this phenomenon is illustrated in Figures 9.2 and 9.3. Both of these hypothetical trades were created on August 15, 2012 with Google (GOOG) trading at $668. Figure 9.2 shows the risk/reward graph for the Sept/Oct $670 call calendar with a debit of $1,135, an estimated maximum profit of 8%, and a break-even range of $655 to $686. I am estimating the maximum gain from the time decay curve two thirds of the way to expiration at a stock price of $670.

Figure 9.2
Title: GOOG Sept/Oct $670 Call Calendar Spread
Source: *Screenshots provided courtesy of Optionetics Platinum © 2014. All rights reserved, etc.*

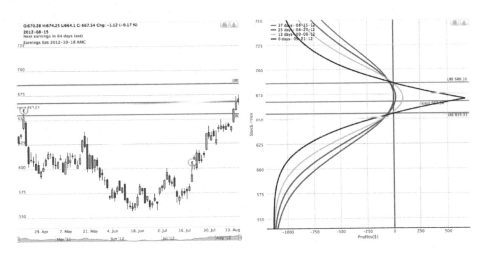

On the same date we could have placed the Oct/Nov $670 call calendar for a debit of $485, with an estimated maximum profit of 60% and a break-even range of $634 to $711 (Figure 9.3).

The break-even range of the October/November spread has more than doubled from $31 to $77 and the profitability has jumped from a weak 8% return to 60%. Why is there such a dramatic difference in these calendar spreads? The answer lies with the volatility skew. The Sept/Oct $670 call calendar of Figure 9.2 has a negative volatility skew of over 5 points. Some authors cite skews as a percentage difference in the two values of implied volatility; I simply cite the difference in percentage points, i.e., 23.9 − 18.6 = 5.3. The October calls have a much higher implied volatility than the September calls because the market was already looking forward to Google's earnings announcement on October 18th, so the October calls were already starting to be bid up in price. With the Oct/Nov $670 call calendar, we are selling the expensive options and we have a positive implied volatility skew of almost one point. That leads to a larger break-even range and greater profit potential.

Figure 9.3
GOOG Oct/Nov $670 Call Calendar Spread
Source: *Screenshots provided courtesy of Optionetics Platinum* © *2014. All rights reserved, etc.*

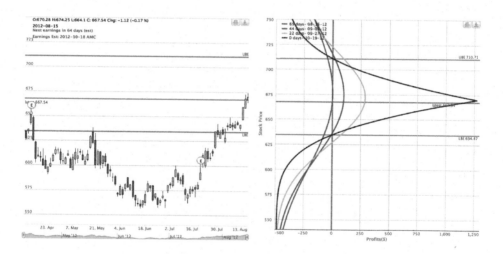

Larger positive volatility skews broaden the break-even range and increase the position's potential profitability. However, that larger positive skew is accompanied by a larger risk of price movement, so there is always a trade-off.

When managing a calendar spread, it is imperative that the trader monitor the implied volatility of each option leg in the position. On some occasions, the position may begin with a positive volatility skew, but then begin to deteriorate, creating a negative volatility skew. The vega of our long option is always larger than the short option (vega increases with time). Thus, increasing implied volatility may have a positive effect on our position even though the absolute amount of the increase in implied volatility in the long option is less than the short option. But if implied volatility for our short option has increased by one point and implied volatility of our long option is flat or decreasing, our calendar is likely losing money.

We are left with three critical lessons for our calendar spreads:

> Always ensure the stock or index's implied volatility is in the bottom quartile of its historical levels of implied volatility before establishing the calendar spread.
> Check the volatility skew. Trade from a neutral or a small positive skew.
> Vega risk is the primary risk of the calendar spread; monitor implied volatility changes in each option leg closely while in the calendar spread trade. If implied volatility decreases or a positive volatility skew begins to develop, close the position.

The Search For Candidates

The directional trader's search for calendar spread candidates is different from that of the non-directional trader. Good candidates for the directional trader will be stocks he expects to trade within a relatively narrow range over the near future.

The non-directional trader will predominantly use broad market indexes for her calendar spreads. Excellent candidates include the Standard and Poors 500 Index (SPX), the Standard and Poors 100 Index (XEO), the NASDAQ 100 Index (NDX) and the Russell 2000 Index (RUT). XEO is a European style option on the Standard and Poors 100 Index whereas OEX is the American style option on the Standard and Poors 100 Index.

For the non-directional trader with a smaller account, using the corresponding Exchange Traded Fund (ETF) will enable trades with much less capital at risk. Earlier in this chapter, we considered the SPX Aug/Sep $1985 call calendar spread. Ten contracts of that SPX call calendar spread would require a debit of $13,550. SPY is the ticker symbol for the corresponding Standard and Poors 500 ETF. The ten contract position of the SPY Aug/Sep $198 call calendar spread would cost $1,380 to establish, or approximately ten percent of the capital required for the SPX trade. Similarly, options on the Russell 2000 ETF (IWM) could be used instead of options on the Russell 2000 Index (RUT) or options on the NASDAQ 100 ETF (QQQ) could be used instead of options on the NASDAQ 100 Index (NDX). As the account balance grows, one would shift to the index options due to increasing commission costs for the larger number of contracts being traded in the ETF options.

However, as we noted in the previous section, the vega risk of the calendar spread should always be paramount in your mind as you look for potential trade candidates. Current levels of implied volatility must be historically low; in that way you have put the probabilities on your side – in those cases, implied volatility is more likely to rise rather than drop.

The following approach is recommended for the non-directional trader searching for a good candidate for the ATM calendar spread:

1. Select from the broad market indexes: SPX, XEO, NDX, and RUT.
2. Sell about 30 days of time premium to maximize the time decay.
3. Check the current value of implied volatility and its history over the past year. Be sure implied volatility is in the lower quartile of its recent history. This is critical; if this condition isn't satisfied, stop here.
4. Check the volatility skew:
   a) Don't trade a negative skew of one point or more.
   b) If the positive skew is greater than 4 points, don't enter the position at this time.
5. Ensure that no earnings announcements or other significant events are expected over the next thirty days. Some traders may use the calendar spread to benefit from increasing implied volatility in advance of an earnings announcement. But that position must be closed before the announcement; this is a more speculative use of the calendar spread.

6. View the risk/reward graph in your options analysis software; be sure the break-even range is centered on the current price of the index. If it is skewed one way or the other, consider a double calendar (more in the following chapter).

Again, I must emphasize that steps three and four in the process above are critical. Vega risk is the largest downside risk facing this trade. Ensuring your position is starting at a low level of implied volatility and that the volatility skew is either neutral or positive are crucial factors for success when trading the calendar spread. In my experience, the losses that occur when a large price move occurs are much smaller than the losses due to a drop in implied volatility or the development of a positive volatility skew while in the trade.

Trade Management and Adjustment

Enter your order for the calendar spread at the midpoint of the bid/ask spread. If the order isn't filled within 1-2 minutes, adjust the limit price upward by two to three cents; continue this process until the order fills. Be patient; every nickel counts.

Write the following in your trading journal:

> ➢ Stop loss prices (set at the break-even prices or slightly beyond).
> ➢ Set an over-riding stop loss of 25% on the position.
> ➢ Set a profit stop of 50% of the maximum potential gain that is predicted by your options analysis software one week before expiration. When that point is hit, close half of the contracts. Close the balance of the contracts if the gains begin to decline.
> ➢ Watch the ATM implied volatility of the index carefully; if implied volatility decreases two percentage points, close the trade.
> ➢ Monitor the implied volatility of the individual legs; if a positive volatility skew develops, close the trade.
> ➢ The time stop is the Friday before expiration week; close the position.

Until you gain some experience with calendar spreads, simply close the spreads when the price trips one of the break-even prices or the position stop loss is exceeded. In fact, many experienced traders do not adjust the calendar spread; they just follow the stop loss guidelines outlined above.

If you choose to adjust your calendar spread, use the break-even prices as your adjustment triggers. When the stock or index price hits one of the adjustment triggers, close half of your spreads and open an equal number of new calendar spreads at a strike price close to the current index price. For example, if we opened ten contracts of a $198 call calendar on SPY when it was trading at $198, and SPY has now traded down to $194 and crossed our lower break-even price at $195, we would close 5 contracts of the $198 call calendars and open 5 contracts of the $194 put calendars. If SPY had moved up in price, we would establish the new calendar spreads with call options.

Don't adjust the calendar spread if you have less than 15 days left to expiration. In those cases, simply close the position.

Early Exercise

We discussed the aspects of early exercise or assignment of our short option positions within vertical spreads in Chapter 7. Those principles apply to the short option positions within calendar spreads as well, but with some important differences. All stock options may be exercised on any business day prior to expiration. These are known as American style options. European style options may only be exercised at expiration. Most broad index options are European style, e.g., SPX, RUT, and NDX are all European style. The OEX (S&P 100) is a notable exception of an index option with American style exercise. But XEO is the equivalent of OEX with European style of exercise. Be sure you know the specifications of exercise for the options you are trading.

When one is trading calendar spreads on stocks, early exercise of the short front month options is always a possibility, but this only occurs under very specific circumstances. We are at risk for early exercise of our short options when the option is ITM and extrinsic value has diminished to $0.20 or less. In one sense, early exercise of the front month option isn't a concern since the long option in the later month can be exercised to protect the assignment. However, we would lose a significant amount of extrinsic value with the exercise of that later month option so we wish to avoid that scenario.

I recommend the non-directional trader use European style index options for trading the ATM calendar spread. This eliminates one more issue that might result in an ugly surprise during the trade.

OTM Calendar Spreads

While the ATM calendar spread is a classic delta neutral trade, one may place the calendar spread OTM to speculate on a directional move. If I am bullish on a stock, I could place a call calendar spread above the current stock price. OTM calendars are usually inexpensive positions and will dramatically gain in value as the stock price trades upward. If I am bearish on a stock, I could place a put calendar spread below the current stock price. As the stock price trades downward, the put calendar will increase in value.

OTM calendar spreads are speculative trades and therefore are not the focus of this book. But they are the building blocks for the double calendar spread, a powerful non-directional trade, and the subject of our next chapter.

Summary

The calendar spread, placed at the money (ATM) is an excellent non-directional trade. This trade may be used with individual stocks or broad market indexes. When played on individual stocks, one may use stocks whose options have relatively low or relatively high values of implied volatility. Stocks with low levels of implied volatility will carry smaller option premiums and therefore lower returns, but the price movement risk (or delta risk) is minimized. Higher implied volatility stocks offer larger returns and a broader range of profitability, but with higher delta risk. In either case, it is imperative that the current implied volatility is relatively low when compared to that stock or index's past history of implied volatility.

Calendar spreads carry a risk of loss due to either an extreme price move in either direction or a decrease in implied volatility. This volatility risk is referred to as vega risk. Calendar spreads always have large positive vega values; thus, decreasing implied volatility will hurt the position's profitability. Vega risk is the larger of the two principal risk sensitivities for the calendar spread. Monitoring the calendar spread should include 1) confirming that the underlying stock or index price remains within the break-even prices of the position, and 2) monitoring the values of implied volatility for each leg.

Non-directional traders will position the ATM calendar spread on a broad market index with a neutral or slightly positive implied volatility skew. Conservative traders will close the position if the underlying price reaches either break-even price. Aggressive traders may adjust their position by closing a portion of the original spreads and opening an equal number of new calendar spreads near the current underlying price if sufficient time remains before expiration.

All calendar spread traders should monitor the implied volatility of each leg of the spread and close the trade if implied volatility of either option drops by more than one point. The trade should also be closed if a positive volatility skew develops in the course of the trade.

CHAPTER TEN

DOUBLE CALENDAR SPREADS

The double calendar spread is formed when an OTM call calendar is positioned above the stock price and an OTM put calendar is positioned below the stock price. Each of these trades is a speculative, directional trade. But when used together, these speculative, directional trades form a delta neutral, non-directional trade. When should we use a double calendar instead of the ATM calendar?

Single Or Double?

Figure 10.1 displays the risk/reward graph for the Google Aug/Sep $590 call calendar on July 15th, 2014 with Google trading at $593. The debit to create the spread is $485, the break-even range is $559 to $626, and the ATM return about a week before expiration is estimated at 70%.

Compare the Google ATM calendar spread in Figure 10.1 with the Google Aug/Sep 585/615 double calendar spread in Figure 10.2. The double calendar requires a larger investment of $855 and consequently, a somewhat smaller estimated ATM return of about 59%. But the break-even range is about 24% wider: $551 to $634.

These examples illustrate the principal differences between the calendar spread and the double calendar spread:

➤ The double calendar spread has a larger break-even range, and thus may tolerate larger price moves in the underlying stock or index.

➤ The ATM calendar spread typically has a larger potential return because we are selling the ATM options.

Figure 10.1
GOOGL Aug/Sep $590 Call Calendar Spread
Source: *Screenshots provided courtesy of Optionetics Platinum © 2014. All rights reserved, etc.*

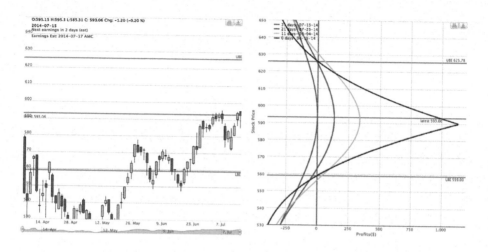

Figure 10.2
GOOGL Aug/Sep 585/615 Double Calendar Spread
Source: *Screenshots provided courtesy of Optionetics Platinum © 2014. All rights reserved, etc.*

When the directional trader is using the ATM calendar spread on a stock, he may prefer a double calendar if the underlying stock has higher implied volatility. For example, if one were trading calendar spreads on Google and saw that the ATM implied volatility was 35%, we would consider this to be historically low for this stock. But in the larger stock universe, this is a relatively high volatility stock. Implied volatility of 35% for General Electric would be historically high for that stock. The high volatility corresponds to a higher risk of price movement and the double calendar's larger break-even range will better accommodate those price moves.

The double calendar spread is the preferred choice for the lower volatility stock when the stock price is in between strike prices. The double calendar will be more delta neutral than the calendar spread formed with the options on either side of the stock price. The option premium in low volatility stocks drops off dramatically as we move OTM, so the strike prices used in the double calendar on a low volatility stock may only be $5 or $10 apart.

When the non-directional trader is using the double calendar spread on a broad market index, she may prefer the double calendar spread to an ATM calendar spread because of the broader break-even range.

The Search For Candidates

The approach we use for finding a good candidate for the double calendar spread is very similar to what we had with the ATM calendar; the main difference is the search for the optimal strike prices. Either stocks or broad market index options may be used. I prefer index options for non-directional trading, because we eliminate individual stock risk.

1. Sell about 30 days of time premium to maximize the time decay.
2. Check the current value of implied volatility and its history over the past year. Be sure implied volatility is in the lower quartile of its recent history. This is critical; if this condition isn't satisfied, stop here.
3. Check the volatility skew:

a) Don't trade a negative skew of one point or more.

b) If the positive skew is greater than 4 points, investigate very carefully. The market is expecting something.

4. Ensure that no earnings announcements or other significant events are expected over the next thirty days. Some traders may use the double calendar to benefit from increasing implied volatility in advance of an earnings announcement. That position must be closed before the announcement; this is a more speculative use of the double calendar.

5. The double calendar spread is built with OTM options. Ensure you are selling at least $0.50 of time value in the front month; otherwise, trading commissions take too much of your profit.

6. View the risk/reward graph in your option analysis software; experiment with different strike prices to find the optimum risk/reward graph. Minimize or eliminate any droop in the risk/reward curve.

7. Estimate the likely return from the risk/reward graph if you close the trade one week before expiration. Be sure this is at least 30%. Disregard the return at expiration; that return is unrealistic because we won't be taking the trade into expiration week.

Determining The Optimal Strike Prices

Positioning the strike prices of the double calendar spread involves trade-offs between the break-even range, the debit required to establish the position, and the estimated profitability. Once we have found a good candidate for the double calendar spread, we plot the risk/reward graph for varying strike prices, starting on either side of the stock or index price and moving farther OTM. Figures 10.3 through 10.7 show our search for the optimal strike prices for a double calendar spread on SPX.

As we push the strike prices farther apart, we decrease the debit and broaden our break-even range. These are both favorable trends, but our expected gain is decreasing. As we push the strike prices farther OTM, the risk/reward curves begin to droop in the middle and our profitability decreases and may also become skewed to one side or the other. Table 10.1 summarizes this search for the optimal strike prices for the SPX double calendar spread on July 15th, 2014 with SPX at $1973. The 1970/1980 spread has the highest potential return but has a rather narrow break-even range. And it is easy to throw out the 1930/2020 spread because the risk/reward curves have both drooped and and skewed toward the upside; this results in not only a lower return ATM, but a possible loss at lower prices within the break-even range. The optimal choice is somewhat a matter of the trader's style and risk tolerance, but the choice would probably narrow down to either the 1955/1995 spread or the 1960/1990 spread.

Table 10.1
Trade-Offs With Strike Price Selection

Strike Prices	Debit to Open	Break-Evens	Estimated ATM Return
1970/1980	$2,600	$1945 - $2008	29%
1960/1990	$2,545	$1941 - $2010	23%
1955/1995	$2,505	$1934 - $2012	21%
1945/2005	$2,365	$1929 - $2017	15%
1930/2020	$2,060	$1908 - $2030	5%

Figures 10.3 through 10.7 illustrate this search for the optimal strike prices. The estimated ATM returns in Table 10.1 come from the green curves in the risk/reward diagrams at ten days to expiration, close to the time stop that will trigger on the Friday before expiration week.

Figure 10.3
Title: SPX Aug/Sep 1970/1980 Double Calendar Spread
Source: *Screenshots provided courtesy of Optionetics Platinum © 2014. All rights reserved, etc.*

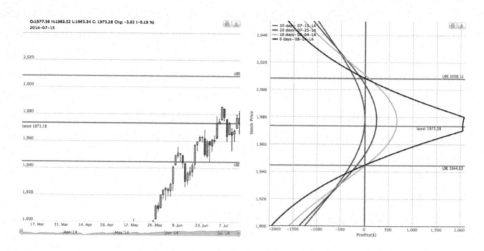

Figure 10.4
Title: SPX Aug/Sep 1960/1990 Double Calendar Spread
Source: *Screenshots provided courtesy of Optionetics Platinum © 2014. All rights reserved, etc.*

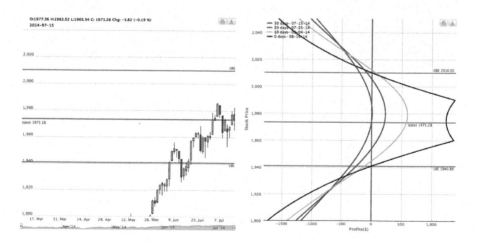

Figure 10.5
SPX Aug/Sep 1955/1995 Double Calendar Spread
Source: *Screenshots provided courtesy of Optionetics Platinum © 2014. All rights reserved, etc.*

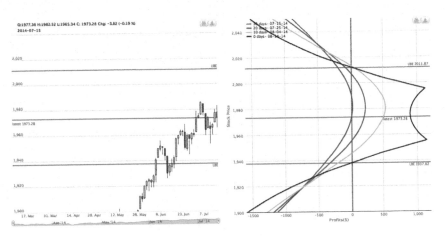

Figure 10.6
SPX Aug/Sep 1945/2005 Double Calendar Spread
Source: *Screenshots provided courtesy of Optionetics Platinum © 2014. All rights reserved, etc.*

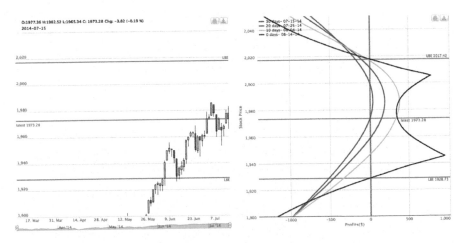

Figure 10.7
SPX Aug/Sep 1930/2020 Double Calendar Spread

Source: *Screenshots provided courtesy of Optionetics Platinum* © *2014. All rights reserved, etc.*

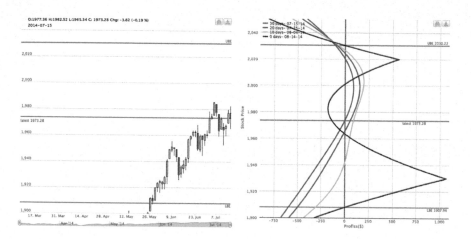

Trade Management and Adjustment

When the double calendar is initiated, write down the following points in your trading journal:

> ➤ Stock or index strike prices and expiration months.
> ➤ Initial debit and break-even prices.
> ➤ Volatility skews for the call and put spreads.
> ➤ Initial position delta.
> ➤ ATM implied volatility for the stock or index.
> ➤ Stop loss: use a 25% loss on the overall position.
> ➤ Volatility stop: if the ATM implied volatility decreases by two percentage points or more, close the trade. If a positive volatility skew develops on either side of the position, close the trade.
> ➤ Adjustment trigger: Activate the adjustment at the break-even prices.

Adjusting the double calendar involves considerable judgment. Once the trigger price has been tripped, evaluate the overall market trend and the stock or index price chart. Determine your estimate of the probability for a further move in the direction that has triggered the adjustment.

If your assessment is neutral to mildly bullish or bearish, then adjust by closing spreads on the offending side and opening new spreads ATM. The new spreads should be call calendars if the stock or index is moving upward against your position or put calendars if it is moving downward. Determine the number to be rolled by modeling the trade with your options analysis software. Your objective is to cut the position delta in half. A good rule of thumb is to close half of the original spreads and open an equal number of new calendar spreads.

If your assessment is strongly bullish or bearish, then close all of the spreads on the offending side and open new spreads above or below the current stock or index price.

If less than fifteen days to expiration remain, and the double calendar is between the front month and the next month, and the trigger for adjustment is tripped, simply close the trade. If the double calendar is over multiple months, e.g., a September/January spread, then make your adjustment as above but roll out the front month to the next expiration month.

As you begin to trade ATM calendars and double calendars, I recommend you trade them in a very simple way with no adjustments whatsoever. Follow the stop loss and volatility stops, and treat the adjustment triggers as stops. This will close out trades more frequently, but will also greatly simplify the trade management process. As you gain experience, you may begin to adjust the positions as described above, but many experienced traders successfully trade these positions without adjustments. Simpler is often better.

Summary

The double calendar spread is formed with an OTM call calendar above the stock price and an OTM put calendar below the stock price. This forms a delta neutral, non-directional trade. The double calendar spread has a larger break-even range and thus may tolerate larger price moves in the underlying stock or index. On the other hand, the ATM calendar spread typically has a larger potential return because we are selling the ATM options.

The double calendar spread is the preferred choice for the lower volatility stock when the stock price is in between strike prices. The non-directional trader may prefer the double calendar spread to an ATM calendar spread because of the broader break-even range.

Positioning the strike prices of the double calendar spread involves trade-offs between the break-even range, the debit required to establish the position, and the estimated profitability. As we push the strike prices farther apart, we decrease the debit and broaden our break-even range, but we also decrease the potential returns.

As you begin to trade ATM calendars and double calendars, I recommend you trade them in a very simple way with no adjustments whatsoever. Follow the stop loss and volatility stops and treat the adjustment triggers as stops. Many experienced traders successfully trade the double calendar without adjustments.

CHAPTER ELEVEN

BUTTERFLY SPREADS

A butterfly spread is created by selling two options at one strike price, moving up one or more strikes and buying one option, and moving down one or more strikes and buying one option. The butterfly can be created with calls or puts. The two sold options are called the "body" of the butterfly and the two long options are the "wings" of the butterfly. The distance between the options sold and the long options on either side must be equal to maintain a margin requirement of zero. Butterfly spreads are quite versatile and may be used in speculative directional trading or for non-directional trading for income generation. Similar to calendar spreads, we may position our butterfly spreads OTM and profit if the underlying stock or index moves in that direction. The ATM butterfly is used either when the trader is predicting a sideways price move, or it may be used by the non-directional trader on a monthly basis as an income generation trading system.

Constructing The Butterfly Spread

If we establish a butterfly with calls, we have effectively put on two vertical spreads. The lower half of the butterfly is a bull call spread while the upper half is a bear call spread; or put another way, we have bought one call spread and sold another call spread where the calls sold in each spread are at the same strike price. Your online broker probably has a butterfly order screen where this entire position may be entered as a single order. Alternatively, you could enter two separate orders for the two vertical spreads that make up the butterfly spread. In my experience, it doesn't make much difference in the cost whether you build the butterfly spread by using a single butterfly order screen or placing two separate vertical spread orders.

We can create a butterfly spread with put options in the same way with one butterfly order or by selling the lower put spread (a bull put spread) and buying the upper put spread (the bear put spread). In this case, the puts sold in both spreads will be at the same strike price.

Figure 11.1 displays the risk/reward graph for a call butterfly spread on the Russell 2000 Index (RUT) on June 15, 2014 with RUT at $1167. This example was constructed by buying one contract of the July $1100 calls and one contract of the July $1230 calls and selling two contracts of the July $1165 calls for a debit of $2,755.

Figure 11.1
RUT ATM Call Butterfly Spread
Source: *Screenshots provided courtesy of Optionetics Platinum © 2014. All rights reserved, etc.*

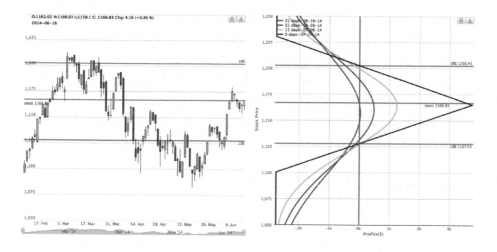

The break-even range is quite broad, from $1128 to $1202. The maximum profit is found at the peak of the risk/reward curve at expiration, at $4,925 or 121%. But this is an unrealistic maximum profit since the index would have to settle precisely at $1165 on expiration Friday for this to occur. A more likely maximum profit estimate is represented by the green time decay line at eleven days to expiration with a profit of about

$1,235 or 45% with RUT at or near $1165. Since we have positioned this butterfly roughly ATM, we refer to this as an ATM butterfly spread.

We could construct the same butterfly with put options. The initial debit of $2,770 is very close to that for the call butterfly in Figure 11.1. The break-even range, estimated profit and the position Greeks are virtually the same for the two positions.

If we increase the width of the butterfly wings by moving the long options farther out from the current index value, we will broaden the break-even range but also increase the initial debit. This will also decrease the maximum return since we have increased the capital at risk.

The profitability of the ATM butterfly derives from the rapid time decay of the ATM options sold. Option time decay accelerates during the last thirty days of the option's life and that powers the profitability of the ATM butterfly. ATM butterflies are appropriate for stocks that are expected to trade within a relatively narrow channel over the next thirty days. Positioning the butterfly spread ATM on a broad market index like SPX, NDX or RUT is a common way to use the butterfly as a non-directional trade for income generation.

The butterfly spread may also be used as a speculative directional trade. Just as we saw when using OTM calendar spreads speculatively, we must have volatility and price predictions. The position vega of the butterfly is negative, so using butterfly spreads to speculate on price moves after an earnings announcement would be a good choice since the spread will not be damaged by the volatility crush after the announcement; in fact, it will appreciate. Whereas the OTM calendar spread would be a better speculative trade when we are expecting an increase in volatility.

Iron Butterfly Spreads

The iron butterfly is created by selling two credit spreads, one with calls and the other with puts; but the two spreads share the same short strike price. In effect, we have sold a call spread just above the current stock or index price and sold a put spread just below the current stock or index price, where the short options in each spread are ATM at the same strike price.

If the wings of the iron butterfly are equidistant, the margin requirement will be based on the spread of one wing, e.g., if our wings are $65 wide, as they are in Figure 11.2, the margin requirement will be $6,500 per contract. However, brokers may have varying margin requirements; you should always confirm your broker's margin requirements before entering a trade.

Figure 11.2 displays the iron butterfly spread on RUT at the same strikes as we used in Figure 11.1. It is difficult to see any differences in these two risk/reward graphs. A comparison of the maximum potential loss, maximum potential gain, and break-even prices of the iron butterfly to those of the call butterfly show the two positions to be virtually identical.

Figure 11.2
RUT ATM Iron Butterfly Spread

Source: *Screenshots provided courtesy of Optionetics Platinum © 2014. All rights reserved, etc.*

This reinforces what we learned in Chapter 7: debit spreads and credit spreads positioned at the same strike prices will have virtually identical returns and risk/reward characteristics. This example with butterfly spreads illustrates the same principle applied to a more complex options strategy.

The butterfly built with all calls or all puts may be called a debit butterfly to distinguish it from the iron butterfly. As we increase the wing span of the debit butterfly (distance between the sold ATM option and the long options on either side), the initial debit increases because one of those long options is moving farther ITM, and therefore is much more expensive. As the capital investment is increasing, our potential return is decreasing. This is a good illustration of the principles we learned in Chapter 2. We are increasing the probability of success as we increase the wing span, but we are decreasing the potential return as well. Our maximum loss for the debit butterfly is the initial debit, so increasing the wing span is also increasing our maximum potential loss. There is a small probability of that loss occurring, but, if it does, it will be large.

These principles from Chapter 2 bear repetition:

> High probability options trades may be considered "conservative" trades.
> But high probability trades always carry a low probability of a relatively large loss.
> A robust system of risk management is essential for success when trading high probability options trades.
> Non-directional income generation trades tend to be high probability trades.

Margin Requirements

When the wings of the debit butterfly spread are equidistant from the body, there is no margin requirement for this trade. However, if the two sold options are pulled apart by even five or ten dollars, the spread will incur a margin requirement for the credit spread side of the butterfly.

We can modify the butterfly in Figure 11.1, resulting in spreads at 1175/1230 and 1100/1155 (Figure 11.3). This is a very similar position, but pulling the two short call strikes apart will create a margin requirement of $5,500 per contract based on the $55 wing width. This butterfly example has an initial debit of $2,670, break-even prices at $1127 and $1203, and an estimated return of about 44%.

Notice that the basic risk/reward characteristics of the butterfly in Figure 11.3 haven't changed much from that of Figure 11.1. The wingspan of the original butterfly was $65, but there was no margin requirement. You might reasonably ask why I would want to modify the debit butterfly in this way – why create a margin requirement? In practice, the non-directional trader may wish to push the two short options to strike prices $5 or $10 apart in cases where the index price falls between strike prices. In this case, the new butterfly will be positioned more delta neutral than choosing the strike price above or below the current index price. Even though a margin requirement has been created, the risk and reward characteristics of the trade have not changed materially. We have positioned our trade to be more delta neutral at the beginning of the trade, but have not sacrificed our potential returns.

Figure 11.3
RUT ATM Call Butterfly Spread (Modified)
Source: *Screenshots provided courtesy of Optionetics Platinum © 2014. All rights reserved, etc.*

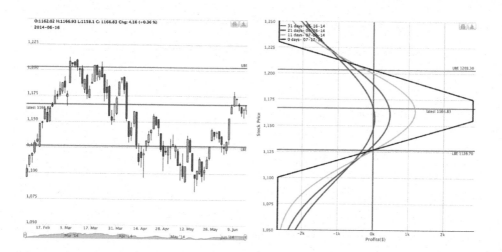

Trade Management And Adjustment

When trading non-directionally, the secret of success is managing the position when the market moves against the trader. Trade management systems range from simple to more complex. Find a trading system that suits your style. Don't think of the more complex adjustments as "advanced". It is true that the more complex adjustments require more experience and more active management of the trade, but those adjustments may not suit your style or be best for your situation.

The trading systems presented here are not presented as the "best" methods to manage the butterfly spread. Each trading system will have its own characteristics, designed by the trader to suit his or her trading style and risk profile. Common aspects of trading systems follow:

> Many trading systems include a profit stop, i.e., a level of profit where the trader closes all or a portion of the spreads. Some traders advocate not having a profit stop and thereby "letting the profits run"; the rebuttal is that taking a gain early eliminates the risk of continuing to be exposed to market events.

> All trading systems include a stop loss, i.e., a level of loss that triggers a close of the entire position.

> All trading systems include a time stop, commonly the Friday before expiration week.

> Some trading systems may include an adjustment technique, accompanied by a trigger that will initiate the adjustment. However, adjustments require time; trades that start around thirty days to expiration often don't have enough time for the adjustment to work.

Four butterfly trading systems follow below with back test results for 2012 and 2013. Pay particular attention to the variation in the returns, but also the pattern of the returns. This illustrates the trade-offs of the choices of parameters when building a trading system.

Butterfly Trade Management System A

The simplest way to non-directionally trade the butterfly spread is to position the debit or iron butterfly spread ATM, with a hard stop loss, a simple profit stop, and a time stop. Many experienced traders manage their butterfly spreads in just this way, so simplicity should not be seen as inferior in any respect.

1. Establish the butterfly spread ATM around 30 days to expiration on one of the broad market indexes: SPX, XEO, NDX or RUT. Position the wings one standard deviation (1σ) away from the options sold ATM.
2. Use your broker's butterfly order form to place the order.
3. Be sure the wings are equidistant to establish a zero margin requirement; the iron butterfly always has a margin requirement.
4. Close the trade when the position is down 20%.
5. Close the trade and take your profit if you are up ≥ 30%.
6. Close the trade on the Friday before expiration week.

Butterfly Trade Management System B

A more conservative butterfly trade management system closes a portion of the position when a minimal level of profit is achieved. We then close the balance of the spreads on any pull back that threatens our gains. This system will cut some gains short but will also minimize losses with a more sensitive stop loss. The end result will likely be smaller gains accompanied by smaller losses, and thus, less volatility in the returns.

1. Establish the butterfly spread ATM around 30 days to expiration on one of the broad market indexes: SPX, XEO, NDX or RUT. Position the wings one standard deviation (1σ) away from the options sold ATM.
2. Use your broker's butterfly order form to place the order.
3. Be sure the wings are equidistant to establish a zero margin requirement; the iron butterfly always has a margin requirement.
4. Close the trade when the position is down 15%.
5. If the position is up ≥ 10%, close half of the spreads; on any pullback that reduces the gains, close the balance of the spreads.
6. Close the trade on the Friday before expiration week.

Butterfly Trade Management System C

We may modify trading system A by simply eliminating the profit stop. This will enable our gains to grow larger in many situations, but there are always trade-offs. This system will allow a nice gain to turn into a loss under the right circumstances.

1. Establish the butterfly spread ATM around 30 days to expiration on one of the broad market indexes: SPX, XEO, NDX or RUT. Position the wings one standard deviation (1σ) away from the options sold ATM.
2. Use your broker's butterfly order form to place the order.
3. Be sure the wings are equidistant to establish a zero margin requirement; the iron butterfly always has a margin requirement.
4. Close the trade when the position is down 20%.
5. No profit stop will be used.
6. Close the trade on the Friday before expiration week.

Butterfly Trade Management System D

We can carry the simple butterfly trade management a step further by establishing the butterfly with a built-in hedge. The following system uses an iron butterfly with wings placed at plus or minus one standard deviation. But, in this case, we buy extra long options on the wings to build in some automatic hedging action. This trading system uses the iron butterfly, built with credit spreads. In theory, one could make a similar adjustment to a debit butterfly, but the extra hedge option on the ITM side of the butterfly would be costly, significantly increasing the initial position debit; that approach really isn't feasible.

1. Establish the iron butterfly spread ATM around 30 days to expiration on one of the broad market indexes: SPX, XEO, NDX or RUT. Position the wings one standard deviation (1σ) away from the options sold ATM.
2. Use your broker's butterfly order form to place the order.
3. Be sure the wings are equidistant to minimize the margin requirement and generate a symmetrical break-even range.

4. Buy an extra call and put on each wing for every ten butterfly spreads, i.e., if I have ten call spreads on one side of the butterfly position, I would buy one extra long call option, and similarly on the put side, I would buy one extra put option.
5. Close the trade when the position is down 20%.
6. Close the trade and take your profit if you are up ≥ 30%.
7. Close the trade on the Friday before expiration week.

Back Testing The Butterfly Trading Systems

Trade management and adjustment systems always have their advantages and disadvantages. Some work better in certain market environments than others. In general, there is no "silver bullet". In this section, we back test the trade management systems outlined above for managing the butterfly spread.

Back testing can be helpful to traders who are considering alternate approaches to their trading system, but one must be aware of the limitations of back testing:

➤ First and foremost, the validity of back testing is limited because we have chosen a particular period of time in history. The trading system we are evaluating may work well in one period of time but not nearly so well in another. It is wise to temper your enthusiasm for very positive back testing results. It is always possible that the market is entering a period of time that will be much less favorable for the trading system under consideration.

➤ The software I used for the back testing uses the daily closing prices for the options. This presents two limitations:

✓ The options prices posted at the close of trading each day often contain errors; during trading hours, mispriced options are self-correcting via arbitrage, but there is no process or incentive to correct closing prices.

✓ The trader will likely have made adjustments or closed spreads intra-day during a large price move. Limiting our back testing to closing prices may accentuate some results, both higher and lower.

I back tested the trading systems of the last section for 2012 and 2013; Figures 11.4 through 11.11 summarize the results. The choice of the particular time period for the back testing is critical to the results. I arbitrarily chose the last two years for back testing these systems simply because I was writing this chapter in the spring of 2014. However, both years may actually have been good years for back testing non-directional strategies. The markets were relatively calm and friendly to non-directional strategies early in 2012, but the markets grew much more volatile in the fall with the presidential elections and fears of the approaching fiscal cliff. 2013 was a strong bull market overall, but exhibited several periods of strong price volatility. It wasn't uncommon to see the market drop two or three percent in seven or eight trading sessions, only to see it reverse and recover all of those losses within just a few sessions. These were difficult years for non-directional traders, so they make good years to use for back testing these systems.

All of these butterfly trading systems showed positive results for both 2012 and 2013 and the results varied with the trading rules selected in each system. But the risk management inherent in each trade management system resulted in positive results for the year in all cases. That may be the most important conclusion to draw from this analysis. Traders will always favor a particular trading system, but successful systems will always contain robust systems for risk management. And all trading systems will perform better or worse in particular market environments. The key to success is a solid risk management system that enables the trader to survive the bad times with minimal losses and build gains in the good times.

Compare the 2012 back testing results for System A of Figure 11.4 to the results of System B in Figure 11.5. System B limits gains by closing half of the spreads when the position is up by 10% and then closes the balance of the spreads on any pullback. This system also limits losses more severely with a 15% stop loss. The net result is smaller gains and also smaller losses for the more conservative system B; one would expect the results over a longer period of time to display a smaller range from the largest gains down to the largest losses. Notice that the more conservative trade management system B results in two losses and ten gains, whereas the relatively simple trade management system A has five losses during the year. Some traders will find less volatility in the results to be more comfortable, but it comes at a price with the net gains for the year at 25% versus the 37% gains of system A. This is principally due to the more conservative profit stop in System B.

Figure 11.4
Butterfly System A Back-Test Results For 2012

Expiration Month	Open Date	Spreads	Initial Credit	Close Date	Reason Closed	Net Return ($)	Net Return (%)	Portfolio Value	Portfolio Return (%)
Jan-12	12/20/11	670/740/810	$40,748	1/5/12	Profit	$10,730	37%	$90,730	13.4%
Feb-12	1/17/12	695/765/835	$39,185	2/1/12	Loss	-$5,910	-19%	$84,820	6.0%
Mar-12	2/14/12	750/820/890	$37,398	3/1/12	Profit	$11,930	37%	$96,750	20.9%
Apr-12	3/20/12	770/830/890	$37,548	4/5/12	Profit	$8,300	37%	$105,050	31.3%
May-12	4/17/12	750/815/880	$34,923	5/3/12	Profit	$9,680	32%	$114,730	43.4%
Jun-12	5/15/12	710/775/840	$38,640	5/29/12	Profit	$9,180	35%	$123,910	54.9%
Jul-12	6/19/12	720/785/850	$34,075	7/10/12	Profit	$10,980	36%	$134,890	68.6%
Aug-12	7/17/12	730/800/870	$34,025	8/6/12	Profit	$14,110	39%	$149,000	86.3%
Sep-12	8/21/12	750/815/880	$28,769	9/13/12	Loss	-$12,880	-36%	$136,120	70.2%
Oct-12	9/18/12	790/855/920	$29,245	10/12/12	Time	-$2,720	-8%	$133,400	66.8%
Nov-12	10/16/12	770/835/900	$29,704	11/8/12	Loss	-$10,280	-29%	$123,120	53.9%
Dec-12	11/20/12	730/795/860	$27,524	12/11/12	Loss	-$13,520	-36%	$109,600	37.0%

Assumes a beginning balance of $80,000.
Trading commissions were not included.
Each butterfly consists of ten RUT contracts.
The wings were positioned at approximately one standard deviation OTM.
The profit stop was ≥ 30%.
The stop loss was ≥ 20%.
The time stop was the Friday before expiration week.

The back testing results for the trading systems A and B in 2013 are presented in Figures 11.6 and 11.7. System A outperformed B in both years, but the more conservative profit stop hurt the results for system B in 2013 more than it did in 2012.

Two lessons are illustrated:

➤ The risk management rules inherent in both trading systems protected against longer term losses in both years for both systems.

> ➤ Trading system results will vary somewhat from year to year. The particular market environment does make a difference. It is easy to pick a favorable time period for any trading system, but that does not guarantee anything about future performance.

Figure 11.5
Butterfly System B Back-Test Results For 2012

Expiration Month	Open Date	Spreads	Initial Credit	Close Half Date	Close Date	Stop Loss?	Time Stop?	Net Return ($)	Net Return (%)	Portfolio Value	Portfolio Return (%)
Jan-12	12/20/11	670/740/810	$40,748	12/28/11	1/13/12		Yes	$9,260	32%	$89,260	11.6%
Feb-12	1/17/12	695/765/835	$39,185	1/23/12	1/24/12			$2,535	8%	$91,795	14.7%
Mar-12	2/14/12	750/820/890	$37,398	2/22/12	3/5/12			$9,120	28%	$100,915	26.1%
Apr-12	3/20/12	770/830/890	$37,548	3/28/12	4/9/12			$3,050	14%	$103,965	30.0%
May-12	4/17/12	750/815/880	$34,923	4/20/12	4/23/12			$2,560	9%	$106,525	33.2%
Jun-12	5/15/12	710/775/840	$38,640	5/21/12	6/1/12			$2,960	11%	$109,485	36.9%
Jul-12	6/19/12	720/785/850	$34,075	6/27/12	6/29/12			$3,330	11%	$112,815	41.0%
Aug-12	7/17/12	730/800/870	$34,025	7/20/12	7/23/12			$2,380	7%	$115,195	44.0%
Sep-12	8/21/12	750/815/880	$28,769	NA	9/13/12	Yes		-$12,880	-36%	$102,315	27.9%
Oct-12	9/18/12	790/855/920	$29,245	9/24/12	9/25/12			$2,650	7%	$104,965	31.2%
Nov-12	10/16/12	770/835/900	$29,704	11/1/12	11/2/12			$2,140	6%	$107,105	33.5%
Dec-12	11/20/12	730/795/860	$27,524	NA	11/79/11	Yes		-$7,230	-19%	$99,875	24.8%

Assumes a beginning balance of $80,000.
Trading commissions were not included.
Each butterfly consists of ten RUT contracts.
The wings were positioned at approximately one standard deviation OTM.
The profit stop was ≥ 10%, close half of the contracts; then close balance on a pullback.
The stop loss was ≥ 15%.
The time stop was the Friday before expiration week.

Trading system C drops the profit stop requirement of system A and the results are displayed in Figures 11.8 and 11.9. This system allows the trader to "let the winners run" and stops out the losses at 20%. This resulted in an extremely good back testing result in 2012 at +70% and a 34% gain for 2013. These time periods for the back testing worked out favorably. In a different time period of back testing, we could have experienced one or more trades where we were up 25-30% and then had the market reverse on us, resulting in a loss when we hit the time stop. Preventing that type of whipsaw is the power of the profit stop, but it comes at the price of locking in today's gains and giving up the possibility of larger returns tomorrow.

Figure 11.6
Butterfly System A Back-Test Results For 2013

Expiration Month	Open Date	Spreads	Initial Credit	Close Date	Reason Closed	Net Return ($)	Net Return (%)	Portfolio Value	Portfolio Return (%)
Jan-13	12/17/12	790/835/880	$27,772	1/2/13	Loss	-$6,979	-41%	$73,021	-8.7%
Feb-13	1/14/13	820/880/930	$27,000	2/1/13	Loss	-$4,910	-21%	$68,111	-14.9%
Mar-13	2/11/13	880/915/950	$22,200	2/28/13	Profit	$3,850	30%	$71,961	-10.0%
Apr-13	3/19/13	890/945/1000	$27,300	4/10/13	Profit	$12,410	45%	$84,371	5.5%
May-13	4/16/13	865/925/985	$30,870	5/6/13	Loss	-$6,410	-22%	$77,961	-2.5%
Jun-13	5/21/13	950/1000/1050	$28,920	6/13/13	Profit	$8,970	43%	$86,931	8.7%
Jul-13	6/18/13	945/1000/1055	$33,550	6/28/13	Profit	$7,180	34%	$94,111	17.6%
Aug-13	7/15/13	995/1045/1095	$30,520	8/2/13	Profit	$6,020	31%	$100,131	25.2%
Sep-13	8/20/13	975/1030/1085	$32,300	9/13/13	Time	$4,650	21%	$104,781	31.0%
Oct-13	9/17/13	1010/1065/1120	$33,450	10/11/13	Time	$5,880	27%	$110,661	38.3%
Nov-13	10/15/13	1020/1080/1140	$36,500	11/1/13	Profit	$10,000	43%	$120,661	50.8%
Dec-13	11/19/13	1050/1100/1150	$31,150	11/26/13	Loss	-$4,800	-26%	$115,861	44.8%

Assumes a beginning balance of $80,000.
Trading commissions were not included.
Each butterfly consists of ten RUT contracts.
The wings were positioned at approximately one standard deviation OTM.
The profit stop was ≥ 30%.
The stop loss was ≥ 20%.
The time stop was the Friday before expiration week.

Figure 11.7
Butterfly System B Back-Test Results For 2013

Expiration Month	Open Date	Spreads	Initial Credit	Close Half Date	Close Date	Stop Loss?	Time Stop?	Net Return ($)	Net Return (%)	Portfolio Value	Portfolio Return (%)
Jan-13	12/17/12	790/835/880	$27,772	NA	1/2/13	Yes		-$6,979	-41%	$73,021	-8.7%
Feb-13	1/14/13	820/880/930	$27,000	NA	2/1/13	Yes		-$6,600	-21%	$66,421	-17.0%
Mar-13	2/11/13	880/915/950	$22,200	2/20/13	2/22/13			$1,405	11%	$67,826	-15.2%
Apr-13	3/19/13	890/945/1000	$27,300	3/28/12	4/3/13			$1,990	7%	$69,816	-12.7%
May-13	4/16/13	865/925/985	$30,870	NA	5/6/13	Yes		-$6,410	-22%	$63,406	-20.7%
Jun-13	5/21/13	950/1000/1050	$28,920	6/3/13	6/4/13		Yes	$2,360	11%	$65,766	-17.8%
Jul-13	6/18/13	945/1000/1055	$33,550	6/27/12	7/8/13			$8,430	39%	$74,196	-7.3%
Aug-13	7/15/13	995/1045/1095	$30,520	7/22/13	7/30/13			$4,390	23%	$78,586	-1.8%
Sep-13	8/20/13	975/1030/1085	$32,300	NA	9/13/13		Yes	$4,650	21%	$83,236	4.0%
Oct-13	9/17/13	1010/1065/1120	$33,450	NA	10/11/13		Yes	$5,880	27%	$89,116	11.4%
Nov-13	10/15/13	1020/1080/1140	$36,500	NA	10/18/13	Yes		-$3,830	-16%	$85,286	6.6%
Dec-13	11/19/13	1050/1100/1150	$31,150	NA	11/22/13	Yes		-$3,030	-16%	$82,256	2.8%

Assumes a beginning balance of $80,000.
Trading commissions were not included.
Each butterfly consists of ten RUT contracts.
The wings were positioned at approximately one standard deviation OTM.
The profit stop was ≥ 10%, close half of the contracts; then close balance on a pullback.
The stop loss was ≥ 15%.
The time stop was the Friday before expiration week.

Figure 11.8
Butterfly System C Back-Test Results For 2012

Expiration Month	Open Date	Spreads	Initial Credit	Close Date	Reason Closed	Net Return ($)	Net Return (%)	Portfolio Value	Portfolio Return (%)
Jan-12	12/20/11	670/740/810	$40,748	1/13/12	Time	$13,410	46%	$93,410	16.8%
Feb-12	1/17/12	695/765/835	$39,185	2/1/12	Loss	-$5,910	-19%	$87,500	9.4%
Mar-12	2/14/12	750/820/890	$37,398	3/9/12	Time	$21,240	65%	$108,740	35.9%
Apr-12	3/20/12	770/830/890	$37,548	4/13/12	Time	$1,730	8%	$110,470	38.1%
May-12	4/17/12	750/815/880	$34,923	5/11/12	Time	$8,300	28%	$118,770	48.5%
Jun-12	5/15/12	710/775/840	$38,640	6/8/12	Time	$22,450	85%	$141,220	76.5%
Jul-12	6/19/12	720/785/850	$34,075	7/13/12	Time	$13,730	44%	$154,950	93.7%
Aug-12	7/17/12	730/800/870	$34,025	8/10/12	Time	$20,580	57%	$175,530	119.4%
Sep-12	8/21/12	750/815/880	$28,769	9/13/12	Loss	-$12,880	-36%	$162,650	103.3%
Oct-12	9/18/12	790/855/920	$29,245	10/12/12	Time	-$2,720	-8%	$159,930	99.9%
Nov-12	10/16/12	770/835/900	$29,704	11/8/12	Loss	-$10,280	-29%	$149,650	87.1%
Dec-12	11/20/12	730/795/860	$27,524	12/11/12	Loss	-$13,520	-36%	$136,130	70.2%

Assumes a beginning balance of $80,000.
Trading commissions were not included.
Each butterfly consists of ten RUT contracts.
The wings were positioned at approximately one standard deviation OTM.
No profit stop.
The stop loss was ≥ 20%.
The time stop was the Friday before expiration week.

Now compare the relatively simple trading system A in Figures 11.4 and 11.6 to System D, a trading system for the iron butterfly, using a built-in hedge at the initiation of the trade (Figures 11.10 and 11.11). It is somewhat surprising that the back testing results for these two systems are very close. Comparing the details reveals the buffering effect of the extra long options in the butterfly in System D. Gains and losses both build more slowly. When the market trends favorably, we see the gains of the hedged system are slightly lower due to the increased initial investment in the hedge options. When the market moves against the position, the hedge options buffer that loss somewhat. The reader may find this result surprising. Building a hedge into the butterfly results in a slower moving position, but does not necessarily deliver superior results in the long term. In both years back-tested, we see that the hedged butterfly trades of system D slightly underperform system A. The advantage of trading system D would be a slower moving position profit and loss figure; this internal hedging may enable the trader to sleep better, but doesn't necessarily improve performance.

Figure 11.9
Butterfly System C Back-Test Results For 2013

Expiration Month	Open Date	Spreads	Initial Credit	Close Date	Reason Closed	Net Return ($)	Net Return (%)	Portfolio Value	Portfolio Return (%)
Jan-13	12/17/12	670/740/810	$40,748	1/2/13	Time	$13,410	46%	$93,410	16.8%
Feb-13	1/14/13	695/765/835	$39,185	2/1/13	Loss	-$5,910	-19%	$87,500	9.4%
Mar-13	2/11/13	750/820/890	$37,398	3/8/13	Time	-$4,009	-31%	$83,491	4.4%
Apr-13	3/19/13	770/830/890	$37,548	4/12/13	Time	$14,680	53%	$98,171	22.7%
May-13	4/16/13	750/815/880	$34,923	5/11/12	Loss	-$6,410	-22%	$91,761	14.7%
Jun-13	5/21/13	710/775/840	$38,640	6/7/13	Time	$5,040	24%	$96,801	21.0%
Jul-13	6/18/13	720/785/850	$34,075	7/12/13	Time	-$2,764	-13%	$94,037	17.5%
Aug-13	7/15/13	730/800/870	$34,025	8/9/13	Time	$15,430	79%	$109,467	36.8%
Sep-13	8/20/13	750/815/880	$28,769	9/13/13	Time	$4,650	21%	$114,117	42.6%
Oct-13	9/17/13	790/855/920	$29,245	10/11/13	Time	$5,880	27%	$119,997	50.0%
Nov-13	10/15/13	770/835/900	$29,704	11/8/13	Time	$12,450	53%	$132,447	65.6%
Dec-13	11/19/13	730/795/860	$27,524	11/26/13	Loss	-$4,800	-26%	$127,647	59.6%

Assumes a beginning balance of $80,000.
Trading commissions were not included.
Each butterfly consists of ten RUT contracts.
The wings were positioned at approximately one standard deviation OTM.
No profit stop.
The stop loss was ≥ 20%.
The time stop was the Friday before expiration week.

One of the important lessons of this series of back testing is the old adage, *"There's no free lunch"*. As we varied our rules to make the stop loss more conservative or removed the profit stop to let the profits run, we always had a trade-off. There is always a price to pay for the advantage gained.

Another critical success factor of trading is to resist looking back and second guessing yourself. As we back test various sets of trading rules, we may see that waiting a couple of days would have dramatically increased our gains or perhaps turned a loss into a gain. That observation may be valuable for improving our system of rules when we are back testing different trading rules. But when trading in the real world, the danger is that you use the "looking in the rear view mirror" as an excuse to continually modify your trading rules from month to month. This erodes your trading discipline and consistency, and may cause you to break your rules at some point in the future and expose yourself to a larger loss.

Develop your trading system and follow your rules. It is important to evaluate your past trades to learn and improve, but don't fall into the trap of always tweaking the system and, consequently, not really having a system.

Figure 11.10
Butterfly System D Back-Test Results For 2012

Expiration Month	Open Date	Spreads	Initial Credit	Close Date	Reason Closed	Net Return ($)	Net Return (%)	Portfolio Value	Portfolio Return (%)
Jan-12	12/20/11	670/740/810	$40,748	1/5/12	Profit	$10,003	34%	$90,003	12.5%
Feb-12	1/17/12	695/765/835	$39,185	2/1/12	Loss	-$6,378	-21%	$83,625	4.5%
Mar-12	2/14/12	750/820/890	$37,398	3/1/12	Profit	$11,413	35%	$95,038	18.8%
Apr-12	3/20/12	770/830/890	$37,548	4/12/12	Profit	$10,228	46%	$105,266	31.6%
May-12	4/17/12	750/815/880	$34,923	5/3/12	Profit	$9,108	30%	$114,374	43.0%
Jun-12	5/15/12	710/775/840	$38,640	5/29/12	Profit	$8,583	33%	$122,957	53.7%
Jul-12	6/19/12	720/785/850	$34,075	7/10/12	Profit	$10,468	34%	$133,425	66.8%
Aug-12	7/17/12	730/800/870	$34,025	8/6/12	Profit	$13,741	38%	$147,166	84.0%
Sep-12	8/21/12	750/815/880	$28,769	9/13/12	Loss	-$13,108	-36%	$134,058	67.6%
Oct-12	9/18/12	790/855/920	$29,245	10/12/12	Time	-$2,914	-8%	$131,144	63.9%
Nov-12	10/16/12	770/835/900	$29,704	11/8/12	Loss	-$10,333	-29%	$120,811	51.0%
Dec-12	11/20/12	730/795/860	$27,524	12/11/12	Loss	-$13,660	-36%	$107,151	33.9%

Assumes a beginning balance of $80,000.
Trading commissions were not included.
Each butterfly consists of ten RUT contracts plus one extra long call and one extra long put.
The wings were positioned at approximately one standard deviation OTM.
The profit stop was ≥ 30%.
The stop loss was ≥ 20%.
The time stop was the Friday before expiration week.

Closing Butterfly Spreads

Closing butterfly spreads can be a little confusing, especially if you have made adjustments to the trade and no longer have a simple butterfly. As you approach either a time stop, like the Friday before expiration week, or have hit a stop loss trigger, analyze the position for the various closing possibilities. For example, if the index has traded up strongly and broken the upper break-even of your call butterfly spread and you have decided to close the position, you could close the entire butterfly with a butterfly order screen by just entering all of the trades in reverse. The Buy To Open (BTO) orders become Sell To Close (STC) orders, and so on. Another alternative is to only close the portion of the butterfly that is in trouble, viz., in this example where the index has moved up against our call butterfly, we might close the bear call spread portion of the butterfly spread and allow the bull call spread portion to expire ITM at its maximum gain.

Figure 11.11
Butterfly System D Back-Test Results For 2013

Expiration Month	Open Date	Spreads	Initial Credit	Close Date	Reason Closed	Net Return ($)	Net Return (%)	Portfolio Value	Portfolio Return (%)
Jan-13	12/17/12	790/835/880	$26,984	1/2/13	Loss	-$6,899	-38%	$73,101	-8.6%
Feb-13	1/14/13	820/880/930	$27,625	2/8/13	Time	-$6,937	-21%	$66,164	-17.3%
Mar-13	2/11/13	880/915/950	$21,370	2/28/13	Profit	$3,530	26%	$69,694	-12.9%
Apr-13	3/19/13	890/945/1000	$26,780	4/10/13	Profit	$11,941	42%	$81,635	2.0%
May-13	4/16/13	865/925/985	$30,277	5/6/13	Loss	-$6,823	-23%	$74,812	-6.5%
Jun-13	5/21/13	950/1000/1050	$28,107	6/13/13	Profit	$8,362	38%	$83,174	4.0%
Jul-13	6/18/13	945/1000/1055	$32,640	6/28/13	Profit	$6,848	31%	$90,022	12.5%
Aug-13	7/15/13	995/1045/1095	$29,612	8/6/13	Profit	$10,302	51%	$100,324	25.4%
Sep-13	8/20/13	975/1030/1085	$31,435	9/13/13	Time	$3,878	17%	$104,202	30.3%
Oct-13	9/17/13	1010/1065/1120	$32,775	10/11/13	Time	$5,263	24%	$109,465	36.8%
Nov-13	10/15/13	1020/1080/1140	$35,605	11/1/13	Profit	$9,205	38%	$118,670	48.3%
Dec-13	11/19/13	1050/1100/1150	$30,200	11/26/13	Loss	-$4,760	-24%	$113,910	42.4%

Assumes a beginning balance of $80,000.
Trading commissions were not included.
Each butterfly consists of ten RUT contracts plus one extra long call and one extra long put.
The wings were positioned at approximately one standard deviation OTM.
The profit stop was ≥ 30%.
The stop loss was ≥ 20%.
The time stop was the Friday before expiration week.

When closing either side of a debit butterfly spread, remember that one half of the butterfly is a debit spread without a margin requirement, but the other side is a credit spread that would have a margin requirement if it were standing alone. If I close the debit spread side of my butterfly spread, I may be surprised to see that a margin requirement has been imposed on the account, possibly limiting the capital available for other trades and adjustments.

Always break down your butterfly spread position into the vertical spread components. This will allow you to better envision the trades required to adjust or close the position. When adjustments have not been made to the position, using the broker's butterfly spread order form to close the entire position may be the simplest and best alternative.

Summary

Butterfly spreads are powerful and versatile trades. In this chapter, we have focused on using the ATM butterfly as a classic non-directional trade that could be used month after month as an income generation strategy. Butterfly spreads may be configured in several different ways; if we use all calls or puts, we have a debit butterfly. Increasing the wingspan will increase the range over which the butterfly is profitable, but it also increases the initial debit, thereby reducing the ultimate return on the capital invested.

The probability of success for these trades tends to be moderately high, e.g., 60-70%. Higher probability trades will have lower probabilities of the loss occurring, but the relative magnitude of that loss, should it occur, will be large. Thus, risk management plays a critical role in the success of the butterfly trade. We evaluated the advantages and disadvantages of several trading systems for the butterfly. Relatively simple systems of rules can be used to successfully trade the butterfly or iron butterfly spread.

Back testing the four trading systems presented in this chapter demonstrated the effects of different trading rules and varying the parameters for those rules. Trading rules should be adjusted and back tested not only to optimize the trading system's profitability, but also to suit the risk profile and trading style of the trader.

The back testing in this chapter also underscores a key point from Chapter 3. The risk management included in each trade management system back tested in this chapter resulted in positive results in all cases (at least over the time period tested). Risk management is the critical success factor in trading.

CHAPTER TWELVE

DOUBLE DIAGONALS

The vertical spread is formed by buying and selling options in the same expiration month. We may diagonalize that spread by buying and selling the two options in different months and at different strike prices. Similar to a double calendar spread, we may establish two diagonal spreads, one positioned above the current index or stock price, and one positioned below the current index or stock price. This is the double diagonal spread, a non-directional option trading strategy.

Building The Double Diagonal Spread

All of the vertical spreads we studied in Chapter 7 may be diagonalized. The double diagonal spread is created from the diagonalized bear call spread and the diagonalized bull put spread. The double diagonal spread is similar to the iron condor where we sell a credit spread above the current stock or index price and another credit spread below the current stock or index price. The difference with the double diagonal is that we are selling our options in the front month and buying the corresponding options in the next month out in time.

On July 15th, 2014, SPX closed at $1973 and we could establish a diagonalized bear call spread by selling the August 2000 call and buying the September 2010 call. Standing by itself, this position is a bearish directional trade that profits by SPX remaining below $2000 before August expiration. We can create the non-directional double diagonal position by adding the diagonalized bull put spread by selling the August 1960 put and buying the September 1950 put. The total debit to establish this position is $1,735 per contract. That might be a little surprising since we normally collect credits for the bear call spread and the bull put spread. But the options we are purchasing in September are much more expensive than the corresponding options we are selling in August; thus, double diagonals are always debit spreads.

The risk/reward graph for this position with one contract is shown in Figure 12.1 with a debit of $1,735, break-even prices at $1941 and $2015, and an estimated ATM return of 32%.

Figure 12.1
SPX Aug/Sep 1950/1960 and 2000/2010 Double Diagonal Spread

Source: *Screenshots provided courtesy of Optionetics Platinum © 2014. All rights reserved, etc.*

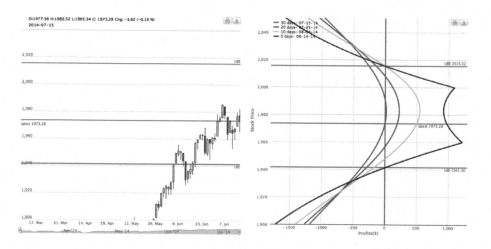

As mentioned earlier, the double diagonal is a debit spread due to the high cost of the long options in the next month. However, this position will invoke a margin requirement from your broker, even though it is a debit spread. The margin requirement may vary from broker to broker, but commonly will be the value of the spread on each side, e.g., two ten dollar diagonal spreads would have a margin requirement of $2,000.

The iron condor will be the subject of the next chapter and consists of an OTM bear call spread and an OTM bull put spread. Brokers commonly only margin one side of the iron condor, e.g., a one contract iron condor formed with ten dollar spreads would have a margin requirement of $1,000. But the double diagonal is not recognized as an "official" options strategy by FINRA, an industry regulatory body, so each diagonal spread is margined individually. This presents a serious disadvantage to the double diagonal since the returns are effectively cut in half by this margin requirement.

The general shape of the risk/reward curve in Figure 12.1 is very similar in shape to the double calendar spread. Establishing a double diagonal spread is also similar to the double calendar in the strike selection process. As we move the strikes OTM, the break-even range increases, but the risk/reward curves begin to droop in the middle and the potential profit decreases. The process of selecting the optimal strike prices for positioning the two spreads is identical to the discussion in Chapter 10 for positioning the spreads of the double calendar, so I won't repeat that here.

The double diagonal is a delta neutral trade and makes its money through its positive theta, or time decay, similar to the double calendar spread. The double diagonal is also a positive vega spread, but not as large a positive vega as we have with the double calendar. So decreases in implied volatility are not as large a concern for the double diagonal, but they can't be ignored.

Trade Management And Adjustment

The double diagonal spread can be used on the broad indexes as an income generation trade. But one must carefully manage the risk to ensure long-term success with the double diagonal spread.

The double diagonal spread is a positive vega position. Hence, this trade shares a risk factor with calendars and double calendar spreads: decreasing implied volatility will seriously harm the profitability of this position. Therefore, always monitor the implied volatility of each leg in the position and close the trade if implied volatility declines.

Always use a simple stop loss on the entire position. I suggest 25% but conservative traders might use 20%. Monitor the profit and loss of your position daily. Whenever the loss exceeds 25% of the risk capital, close the trade. Much of the capital in this trade is tied up in the long options and we may reasonably expect to sell those at the end of the trade and recover much of that capital. Normally, we would regard the margin requirement as the capital at risk in our trade, but that overstates the risk for the double diagonal since both sides are margined. For a double diagonal with ten dollar spreads, that amounts to $2,000 per contract. A conservative trader may consider the total margin requirement as the capital at risk. A more realistic estimate of the capital at risk is the amount of one of the spreads plus the initial debit, e.g., two $10 spreads with a $560 debit could be estimated as about $1,560 of capital at risk. But the broker's margin requirement will be the full $2,000.

Adjustment of the double diagonal is triggered whenever the index price touches one of the short strike prices. Then the trader has a choice of two adjustments:

> One can create a calendar spread on the side being threatened by buying back the short option in the front month and selling the next strike higher or lower to create a calendar spread on that side of the trade.

> Alternatively, one can create a double calendar on the side being threatened by buying the same strike in the later month that we are short in the front month to create one calendar. The other calendar is then created by selling the option at the next strike up or down in the front month.

Assume the example we used above: the Standard and Poors 500 Index (SPX) stands at $1735 and we establish an Aug/Sep 1950/1960 put and 2000/2010 call double diagonal. If SPX trades up to $2000, we can adjust in one of two ways:

1. Create a call calendar at $2010 by buying back the short Aug $2000 call and selling the Aug $2010 call.
2. Create a double calendar at $2000 and $2010 by buying a Sep $2000 call and selling an Aug $2010 call.

Refer back to Chapters 9 and 10 on how to manage and adjust the calendar or double calendar spreads on this side of the position.

These adjustments for the double diagonal spread are a bit more complicated, but they work very well. Paper trade these spreads and adjustments to become more familiar with the adjustments before going live.

The double diagonal spread can be positioned on one of the broad market indexes as a non-directional trade used for monthly income generation. The generalized trading system for initiating and managing the double diagonal is as follows:

1. Initiate the trade with about 30 days to expiration in the front month options.
2. Sell the front month call and put options just inside one standard deviation OTM.
3. Buy the next strike OTM call and OTM put in the next expiration month.
4. Double diagonals are debit spreads due to the high cost of the long options in the next expiration month. But the double diagonal position will have a margin requirement, usually the width of the spread on each side of the trade. Confirm with your broker.
5. Set your stop loss at an overall position loss of > 25%.
6. If the implied volatility of either of the long options in the spread declines by two percentage points or more, close the entire position.
7. If the index price touches either short strike price and less than 15 days are left until expiration, close that side of the trade; if 15 days or more are left until expiration, then adjust the position in one of two ways:
   a) Adjust by buying back the short option and selling the next option OTM, creating a calendar spread on that side of the position, or
   b) Adjust by selling the option in the front month at the strike price where we own the long option in the later month, and buy the option in the later month at the strike price we are short in the front month. This creates a double calendar spread on that side of the position.
8. On the Friday before expiration week, close the position.

Some traders may also wish to use a profit stop in their double diagonal trading systems. The simplest profit stop closes the entire position when a specified level of gain is met. A common alternative is a profit stop that triggers closing half of the position and then allows the balance of the trade to run until some other limit is hit.

An alternative time stop is to apply the Two Sigma Rule on the Friday before expiration week: calculate one standard deviation (1 sigma or 1σ) for that remaining week; close either diagonal spread if that short option is less than two standard deviations, or 2σ, OTM.

Back Testing the Double Diagonal

Back testing is a powerful tool available to the trader that is helpful in developing a trading system before "going live". However, back testing has limitations:

➢ First and foremost, the validity of back testing is limited because we have chosen a particular period of time in history. The trading system we are evaluating may work well in one period of time but not nearly so well in another.

➢ The software I used for the back testing uses the daily closing prices for the options. This presents two limitations:

✓ The options prices posted at the close of trading each day often contain errors; during trading hours, mispriced options are self-correcting via arbitrage, but there is no process or incentive to correct closing prices.

✓ The trader will likely have made adjustments or closed spreads intra-day during a large price move, if were trading "live". Limiting our back testing to closing prices certainly accentuates some results, both higher and lower.

I used the past two full years of 2012 and 2013 for back testing several variations on the generalized trading system for the double diagonal discussed in the previous section of this chapter. Figures 12.2 through 12.7 summarize the results. As noted above, the choice of the particular time period for the back testing is critical to the results. 2012 and 2013 may actually have been good years for back testing non-directional strategies. Both years were far from calm, sideways markets and presented severe challenges to non-directional traders.

Figure 12.2
Back Testing the Double Diagonal Spread for 2012

Expiration Month	Open Date	Spreads	Initial Debit	Adjusted?	Reason Closed	Net Return ($)	Net Return (%)	Portfolio Value	Portfolio Return (%)
Jan-12	12/20/11	680/690 780/790	$14,750	no	Time	-$80	-1%	$24,920	-0.3%
Feb-12	1/17/12	710/720 800/810	$12,150	no	Adj Stop	-$3,970	-33%	$20,950	-16.2%
Mar-12	2/14/12	770/780 860/870	$14,550	no	Time	-$1,550	-11%	$19,400	-22.4%
Apr-12	3/20/12	780/790 860/870	$10,700	no	Adj Stop	-$800	-7%	$18,600	-25.6%
May-12	4/17/12	760/770 850/860	$9,950	no	Time	$1,170	12%	$19,770	-20.9%
Jun-12	5/15/12	740/750 810/820	$13,750	yes	Time	$3,550	26%	$23,320	-6.7%
Jul-12	6/19/12	730/740 820/830	$10,200	yes	Stop Loss	-$5,170	-51%	$18,150	-27.4%
Aug-12	7/17/12	750/760 830/840	$12,600	no	Time	-$2,350	-19%	$15,800	-36.8%
Sep-12	8/21/12	770/780 840/850	$9,700	no	Adj Stop	-$2,400	-25%	$13,400	-46.4%
Oct-12	9/18/12	820/830 880/890	$8,550	no	Adj Stop	-$80	-1%	$13,320	-46.7%
Nov-12	10/16/12	800/810 860/870	$10,200	no	Adj Stop	-$670	-7%	$12,650	-49.4%
Dec-12	11/20/12	760/770 820/830	$7,300	yes	Time	$2,150	29%	$14,800	-40.8%

Assumes a beginning balance of $25,000.
Trading commissions were not included.
Each double diagonal consists of ten RUT contracts.
Spreads were positioned at thirty days from expiration with delta of the short option at 20-25.
No profit stop was used.
No implied volatility stop was used.
A 25% stop loss was used.
If RUT touched the short strike and >15 days remained, a calendar was formed on that side.
If RUT touched the short strike and <15 days remained, the position was closed (Adj Stop).
The time stop was the Friday before expiration week.

The trading system used for the first series of back testing reported in Figures 12.2 and 12.3 consisted of the following rules:

- ➤ A beginning account balance of $25,000 is assumed.
- ➤ Each double diagonal consists of ten contracts on the Russell 2000 Index (RUT).
- ➤ The short options of the spreads were positioned at thirty days to expiration with the delta of the short option at approximately 20 to 25.
- ➤ A stop loss of 25% was used.

> If the value of the index touched the short strike price, and at least 15 days remained until expiration, a calendar was formed on that side of the position as an adjustment; if the adjustment was triggered, but less than 15 days remained, the position was closed.
> The time stop was the Friday before expiration week.

Figure 12.3
Back Testing the Double Diagonal Spread for 2013

Expiration Month	Open Date	Spreads	Initial Debit	Adjusted?	Reason Closed	Net Return ($)	Net Return (%)	Portfolio Value	Portfolio Return (%)
Jan-13	12/18/12	800/810 880/890	$6,150	no	Adj Stop	$900	5%	$25,900	3.6%
Feb-13	1/14/13	840/850 910/920	$9,650	no	Time	-$4,010	-20%	$21,890	-12.4%
Mar-13	2/12/13	870/880 940/950	$8,650	no	Time	$130	1%	$22,020	-11.9%
Apr-13	3/19/13	890/900 970/980	$6,500	no	Time	$150	4%	$22,170	-11.3%
May-13	4/16/13	870/880 960/970	$8,450	no	Adj Stop	$800	4%	$22,970	-8.1%
Jun-13	5/21/13	950/960 1030/1040	$8,850	no	Time	$3,470	18%	$26,440	5.8%
Jul-13	6/18/13	940/950 1040/1050	$9,400	no	Time	$170	1%	$26,610	6.4%
Aug-13	7/16/13	990/1000 1080/1090	$12,650	no	Time	-$550	-2%	$26,060	4.2%
Sep-13	8/20/13	970/980 1070/1080	$9,700	no	Time	$1,670	8%	$27,730	10.9%
Oct-13	9/17/13	1010/1020 1100/111(	$9,000	no	Time	$3,650	19%	$31,380	25.5%
Nov-13	10/15/13	1010/1020 1130/114(	$10,600	no	Time	-$680	-3%	$30,700	22.8%
Dec-13	11/19/13	1050/1060 1140/115(	$9,350	yes	Time	-$2,030	-8%	$28,670	14.7%

Assumes a beginning balance of $25,000.
Trading commissions were not included.
Each double diagonal consists of ten RUT contracts.
Spreads were positioned at thirty days from expiration with delta of the short option at 20-25.
No profit stop was used.
No implied volatility stop was used.
A 25% stop loss was used.
If RUT touched the short strike and >15 days remained, a calendar was formed on that side.
If RUT touched the short strike and <15 days remained, the position was closed (Adj Stop).
The time stop was the Friday before expiration week.

The rules above were used for the back testing results of Figure 12.2, resulting in a net loss of 41% in 2012. Only three trades out of the year resulted in positive gains. This system did a little better in 2013 with a +15% return for the year (Figure 12.3). A closer look at the monthly returns reveals the problem. Double diagonals are positive vega trades, so declining implied volatility will hurt the trade.

In Figures 12.4 and 12.5, I added a simple stop based on a decline in implied volatility and this improved the results dramatically for both years.

If the implied volatility of either long option in the double diagonal decreased by two points or more, the trade was closed. This single addition to the rules resulted a break-even for 2012 and resulted in a gain of 27% in 2013. These results still aren't spectacular, but our implied volatility stop resulted in a swing of forty percentage points in the back testing results for 2012 and almost doubled the returns for 2013. This underscores the vega risk inherent in the double diagonal trading strategy.

Figure 12.4
Back Testing the Double Diagonal Spread for 2012

Expiration Month	Open Date	Spreads	Initial Debit	Adjusted?	Reason Closed	Net Return ($)	Net Return (%)	Portfolio Value	Portfolio Return (%)
Jan-12	12/20/11	680/690 780/790	$14,750	no	IV Stop	$130	1%	$25,130	0.5%
Feb-12	1/17/12	710/720 800/810	$12,150	no	IV Stop	-$200	-2%	$24,930	-0.3%
Mar-12	2/14/12	770/780 860/870	$14,550	no	IV Stop	-$100	-1%	$24,830	-0.7%
Apr-12	3/20/12	780/790 860/870	$10,700	no	Adj Stop	-$800	-7%	$24,030	-3.9%
May-12	4/17/12	760/770 850/860	$9,950	no	IV Stop	-$200	-2%	$23,830	-4.7%
Jun-12	5/15/12	740/750 810/820	$13,750	yes	Time	$3,550	26%	$27,380	9.5%
Jul-12	6/19/12	730/740 820/830	$10,200	no	IV Stop	$500	5%	$27,880	11.5%
Aug-12	7/17/12	750/760 830/840	$12,600	no	IV Stop	-$1,600	-13%	$26,280	5.1%
Sep-12	8/21/12	770/780 840/850	$9,700	no	Adj Stop	-$2,400	-25%	$23,880	-4.5%
Oct-12	9/18/12	820/830 880/890	$8,550	no	IV Stop	-$550	6%	$23,330	-6.6%
Nov-12	10/16/12	800/810 860/870	$10,200	no	Adj Stop	-$670	-7%	$22,680	-9.3%
Dec-12	11/20/12	760/770 820/830	$7,300	yes	Time	$2,150	29%	$24,830	-0.7%

Assumes a beginning balance of $25,000.
Trading commissions were not included.
Each double diagonal consists of ten RUT contracts.
Spreads were positioned at thirty days from expiration with delta of the short option at 20-25.
No profit stop was used.
If IV of either long option decreased by ≥ 2 points, the positions was closed (IV Stop).
A 25% stop loss was used.
If RUT touched the short strike and >15 days remained, a calendar was formed on that side.
If RUT touched the short strike and <15 days remained, the position was closed (Adj Stop).
The time stop was the Friday before expiration week.

My next refinement was to add a conservative profit stop and this generated the results in Figures 12.6 and 12.7. The rule was to close the entire position whenever a gain of 5% or more could be achieved. For 2012, this turned two of our losses into gains and pushed the overall results to a positive 11% (Figure 12.6). However, the results for 2013 in Figure 12.7 illustrate the trade-offs of the profit stop. Adding the profit stop helped the results in 2012, improving the break-even to an 11% gain; the profit stop accomplished this improvement by locking in some gains that would turn into losses if they were held until the time stop triggered. But that wasn't the case in 2013; the conservative profit stop reduced the gains in 2013 to +16% from the +27% achieved without a profit stop. A conservative profit stop often reduces the gains by passing up occasional large gains when the profits are allowed to run. All trading rules have trade-offs.

Figure 12.5
Back Testing the Double Diagonal Spread for 2013

Expiration Month	Open Date	Spreads	Initial Debit	Adjusted?	Reason Closed	Net Return ($)	Net Return (%)	Portfolio Value	Portfolio Return (%)
Jan-13	12/18/12	800/810 880/890	$6,150	no	Adj Stop	$900	5%	$25,900	3.6%
Feb-13	1/14/13	840/850 910/920	$9,650	no	IV Stop	-$1,330	-7%	$24,570	-1.7%
Mar-13	2/12/13	870/880 940/950	$8,650	no	Time	$130	1%	$24,700	-1.2%
Apr-13	3/19/13	890/900 970/980	$6,500	no	Time	$150	4%	$24,850	-0.6%
May-13	4/16/13	870/880 960/970	$8,450	no	Adj Stop	$800	4%	$25,650	2.6%
Jun-13	5/21/13	950/960 1030/1040	$8,850	no	Time	$3,470	18%	$29,120	16.5%
Jul-13	6/18/13	940/950 1040/1050	$9,400	no	Time	$170	1%	$29,290	17.2%
Aug-13	7/16/13	990/1000 1080/1090	$12,650	no	IV Stop	-$860	-4%	$28,430	13.7%
Sep-13	8/20/13	970/980 1070/1080	$9,700	no	Time	$1,670	8%	$30,100	20.4%
Oct-13	9/17/13	1010/1020 1100/111(	$9,000	no	Time	$3,650	19%	$33,750	35.0%
Nov-13	10/15/13	1010/1020 1130/114(	$10,600	no	IV Stop	$70	1%	$33,820	35.3%
Dec-13	11/19/13	1050/1060 1140/115(	$9,350	yes	Time	-$2,030	-8%	$31,790	27.2%

Assumes a beginning balance of $25,000.
Trading commissions were not included.
Each double diagonal consists of ten RUT contracts.
Spreads were positioned at thirty days from expiration with delta of the short option at 20-25.
No profit stop was used.
A drop of two points in implied volatility of either long option closed the trade.
A 25% stop loss was used.
If RUT touched the short strike and >15 days remained, a calendar was formed on that side.
If RUT touched the short strike and <15 days remained, the position was closed (Adj Stop).
The time stop was the Friday before expiration week.

This series of back testing reminds us that trading strategies with significant levels of vega risk, such as calendars, double calendars and double diagonals, always require diligent monitoring of implied volatility for successful long-term results.

One of the principal advantages of the double diagonal isn't apparent until one gains some experience with this trade. The long options in the next month have larger deltas and thus, as the index moves against one side of the position, those long options appreciate more rapidly. In effect, this buffers the ill effects of the index moving against the position. That explains why we can wait until the index hits one of the short strikes before adjusting. The losses don't build as rapidly with the double diagonal spread.

Figure 12.6
Back Testing the Double Diagonal Spread for 2012

Expiration Month	Open Date	Spreads	Initial Debit	Adjusted?	Reason Closed	Net Return ($)	Net Return (%)	Portfolio Value	Portfolio Return (%)
Jan-12	12/20/11	680/690 780/790	$14,750	no	IV Stop	$130	1%	$25,130	0.5%
Feb-12	1/17/12	710/720 800/810	$12,150	no	IV Stop	-$200	-2%	$24,930	-0.3%
Mar-12	2/14/12	770/780 860/870	$14,550	no	Profit	$1,180	8%	$26,110	4.4%
Apr-12	3/20/12	780/790 860/870	$10,700	no	Adj Stop	-$800	-7%	$25,310	1.2%
May-12	4/17/12	760/770 850/860	$9,950	no	IV Stop	-$200	-2%	$25,110	0.4%
Jun-12	5/15/12	740/750 810/820	$13,750	yes	Profit	$2,050	15%	$27,160	8.6%
Jul-12	6/19/12	730/740 820/830	$10,200	no	IV Stop	$500	5%	$27,660	10.6%
Aug-12	7/17/12	750/760 830/840	$12,600	no	IV Stop	-$1,600	-13%	$26,060	4.2%
Sep-12	8/21/12	770/780 840/850	$9,700	no	Profit	$1,400	14%	$27,460	9.8%
Oct-12	9/18/12	820/830 880/890	$8,550	no	IV Stop	-$530	-6%	$26,930	7.7%
Nov-12	10/16/12	800/810 860/870	$10,200	no	Adj Stop	-$670	-7%	$26,260	5.0%
Dec-12	11/20/12	760/770 820/830	$7,300	yes	Profit	$1,520	21%	$27,780	11.1%

Assumes a beginning balance of $25,000.
Trading commissions were not included.
Each double diagonal consists of ten RUT contracts.
Spreads were positioned at thirty days from expiration with delta of the short option at 20-25.
A profit stop of +5% was used.
If IV of either long options decreased by ± 2 points, the positions was closed (IV Stop).
A 25% stop loss was used.
If RUT touched the short strike and >15 days remained, a calendar was formed on that side.
If RUT touched the short strike and <15 days remained, the position was closed (Adj Stop).
The time stop was the Friday before expiration week.

The iron condor, discussed in the next chapter, is a very similar trade to the double diagonal, but the long options in the iron condor are in the same month as the short options. Traders with experience with both double diagonals and iron condors discover the internal hedging advantage of the double diagonal in the "school of hard knocks". Those long options, which are one month farther out in time, hedge the position very well. But those traders also are painfully reminded of the disadvantageous margining of the double diagonal. The margin requirement on both sides of the position effectively cuts the returns in half as compared to the iron condor spread.

The back testing results of the double diagonal spreads are generally less than the comparable results for the butterfly spread or the iron condor (Chapter 13). But the natural internal hedging discussed above causes the double diagonal to be a much slower moving trade and hence more amenable to the conservative investor. But we pay for that advantage with lower returns. As Mom said, "There's no free lunch."

Figure 12.7
Back Testing the Double Diagonal Spread for 2013

Expiration Month	Open Date	Spreads	Initial Debit	Adjusted?	Reason Closed	Net Return ($)	Net Return (%)	Portfolio Value	Portfolio Return (%)
Jan-13	12/18/12	800/810 880/890	$6,150	no	Profit	$1,050	6%	$26,050	4.2%
Feb-13	1/14/13	840/850 910/920	$9,650	no	IV Stop	-$1,330	-7%	$24,720	-1.1%
Mar-13	2/12/13	870/880 940/950	$8,650	no	Profit	$1,100	6%	$25,820	3.3%
Apr-13	3/19/13	890/900 970/980	$6,500	no	Profit	$850	5%	$26,670	6.7%
May-13	4/16/13	870/880 960/970	$8,450	no	Profit	$1,350	7%	$28,020	12.1%
Jun-13	5/21/13	950/960 1030/1040	$8,850	no	Profit	$1,100	6%	$29,120	16.5%
Jul-13	6/18/13	940/950 1040/1050	$9,400	no	Time	$170	1%	$29,290	17.2%
Aug-13	7/16/13	990/1000 1080/1090	$12,650	no	IV Stop	-$860	-4%	$28,430	13.7%
Sep-13	8/20/13	970/980 1070/1080	$9,700	no	Profit	$1,320	7%	$29,750	19.0%
Oct-13	9/17/13	1010/1020 1100/111(	$9,000	no	Profit	$1,200	6%	$30,950	23.8%
Nov-13	10/15/13	1010/1020 1130/114(	$10,600	no	IV Stop	$70	1%	$31,020	24.1%
Dec-13	11/19/13	1050/1060 1140/115(	$9,350	yes	Time	-$2,030	-8%	$28,990	16.0%

Assumes a beginning balance of $25,000.
Trading commissions were not included.
Each double diagonal consists of ten RUT contracts.
Spreads were positioned at thirty days from expiration with delta of the short option at 20-25.
The profit stop was ≥ 5%.
A drop of two points in implied volatility of either long option closed the trade.
A 25% stop loss was used.
If RUT touched the short strike and >15 days remained, a calendar was formed on that side.
If RUT touched the short strike and <15 days remained, the position was closed (Adj Stop).
The time stop was the Friday before expiration week.

Double Diagonals vs. Double Calendars

Double diagonal spreads and double calendar spreads are both very effective non-directional trades. Double calendar spreads are large positive vega positions; hence, decreasing implied volatility is a significant risk for that position. Double diagonals have smaller positive vegas and are not as sensitive to decreasing implied volatility. But, as we saw in the back testing of the previous section, one cannot ignore the risk of implied volatility declining when we are trading the double diagonal. In high volatility environments where decreasing implied volatility may be more of a risk, none of the positive vega trades should be used, or at least should only be used with a tight stop for a decline in implied volatility.

Double diagonals require more capital to be invested due to the extra expense of the long options one month out in time plus the margin requirements on both sides of the position. This decreases the return on capital for the double diagonal as compared to double calendars.

The double diagonal presents the trader with more alternatives for fine-tuning and adjustment than the double calendar. However, that very flexibility carries additional complexity for the trader.

In my experience, double diagonals are less popular with income traders, who tend to favor iron condors, butterflies, and double calendars. All four of these non-directional trades will be compared and contrasted in Chapter 14.

Summary

The double diagonal spread is a classic non-directional income generation trade. It is a positive vega position, so the current level of implied volatility relative to its history should be considered. The vega risk of the double diagonal is not as severe as it is for the calendar or double calendar, but it remains a significant risk for the double diagonal spread. Implied volatility levels should be considered before entering the trade and then monitored closely during the trade. Double diagonal spreads, calendar spreads, and double calendar spreads are all positive vega positions and hence are not suitable for high volatility markets.

Double diagonals may be adjusted very effectively by creating a calendar or double calendar spread on the side of the trade under pressure. A major disadvantage of the double diagonal is the fact that the broker margins both sides of the position. This effectively reduces the return on investment by half.

One of the principal advantages of the double diagonal is the larger delta of the long options in the position. This slows the rate of growth of the loss as the index is moving against the position. It effectively provides an internal hedge to the position.

CHAPTER THIRTEEN

CONDORS AND IRON CONDORS

The iron condor is a popular options trading strategy. Many different options educators and authors have popularized this trading strategy. The prospect of establishing an options position each month with a 90% probability of success and collecting a nice income month after month is very attractive. But is that too good to be true? The answer is: "yes and no". In fact, many charlatans have deceived people into thinking this is an easy way to generate income each month with minimal risk. The fact is that anyone can teach you how to establish the iron condor; but managing the trade through various markets and achieving profitability over the long term can be elusive. Successfully trading the iron condor is feasible, but it isn't trivial.

Building The Condor Spread

A condor is formed by buying a call spread below the current price of the stock or index and also selling a call spread above the current price of the stock or index. Selling a call credit spread is sometimes called establishing a bear call spread. We buy an OTM (out of the money) call and move down one strike price and sell an OTM call. Since the call we sold is more valuable than the call we bought, we bring a net amount of cash into our account, i.e., the credit. The call spread we purchase that is positioned below the current price of the stock or index is a debit spread and is often called a bull call spread; the debit of this spread is larger than the credit received for the bear call spread, resulting in a net debit for this condor spread built with call options.

One can also build a condor spread with put options. In that case, we would be buying the put spread positioned above the current price of the stock or index price and selling the put spread down below the current price of the stock or index. Again, the position will result in a net debit. Hence, we can build the condor spread with calls or puts and usually these trades are virtually equivalent. These condors are often referred to as debit condors to distinguish them from the iron condor.

Building The Iron Condor Spread

The iron condor spread is a simple variation on the traditional condor spread; if we sell a call spread above the stock or index price for a credit and also sell a put spread below the stock or index price for a credit, we have created an iron condor spread. When we discussed vertical spreads in Chapter 7, we noted that the debit spread and the credit spread at the same strike prices will have virtually identical levels of risk and reward, i.e., there is no inherent advantage to either spread.

This is also true when we compare and contrast the debit condor and the iron condor spreads. On February 15, 2013, with the Russell 2000 index (RUT) at $923, IV = 15.3% and 62 days to April expiration, I established two condor spreads positioned at $\pm 1\sigma$. Recall that this means plus and minus one standard deviation of projected movement in price based on the current price of RUT, the current implied volatility of RUT, and the number of days to expiration. One condor was created with a credit put spread at 820/830 and a debit put spread at 980/990 for a net debit of $840. The other was an iron condor created with a credit put spread at 820/830 and a credit call spread at 980/990. Figure 13.1 displays the risk/reward graph for the debit put condor and Figure 13.2 displays the risk/reward graph for the iron condor at the same strike prices.

The risk/reward graphs are absolutely identical. Both trades have breakeven prices of $828 and $982; the iron condor has a maximum profit of $160 for a 19% return; the debit put condor also has a maximum profit of $160 for a 19% return. But the iron condor does have one significant advantage.

Figure 13.1
RUT Apr 820/830 980/990 Put Condor Spread

Source: *Screenshots provided courtesy of Optionetics Platinum* © *2014. All rights reserved, etc.*

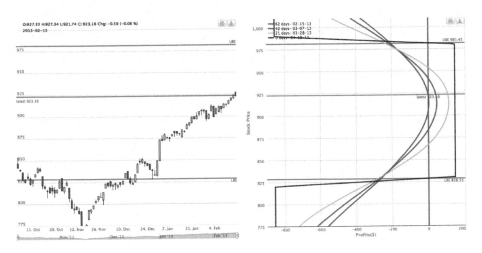

Figure 13.2
RUT Apr 820/830 980/990 Iron Condor Spread

Source: *Screenshots provided courtesy of Optionetics Platinum* © *2014. All rights reserved, etc.*

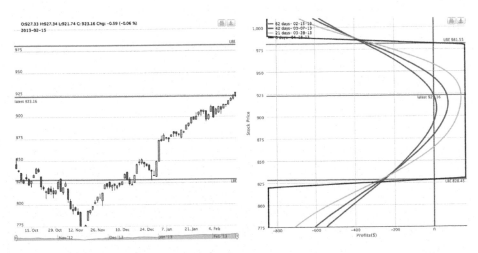

When I establish a vertical spread for a debit, my maximum profit will be achieved when both options are ITM at expiration; then my broker will exercise both options, leaving the amount of the spread in my account. Consider this example: I buy a bull call spread on XYZ at 180/190 for $850 and XYZ closes on expiration Friday at $195. My short $190 calls will be exercised against me, requiring me to sell 100 shares of XYZ at $190. My broker will exercise my $180 calls on my behalf, buying 100 shares of XYZ at $180 and turning around and selling those shares at $190 to satisfy the exercise of my short $190 calls. That leaves the spread between $180 and $190, or $1,000, in my account (less commissions). After subtracting the debit required to establish the spread of $850, I have my net profit of $150.

But consider a similar example with a credit put spread on XYZ at 180/190. If XYZ closes at $195 at expiration, both of my put options expire worthless and I keep my initial credit as my maximum profit. This highlights one of the advantages of the iron condor. Often the trader may allow one or both of the spreads to expire worthless and therefore avoid some additional trading commissions. This will result in some cost savings that translate to additional gains for the iron condor trader over time.

Option brokers assess a margin requirement on credit spreads, but this isn't the margin requirement you may recall from your stock brokerage account. The margin requirement for an option position addresses the "worst case scenario", the maximum loss. If the trader somehow lost more money than was in his account and then disappeared, the broker would have to make up the loss. So the margin requirement for an options trade is effectively a form of escrow that assures the broker that sufficient cash is in the account to cover the maximum loss if it occurs.

Since the iron condor is made up of credit spreads, it will incur a margin requirement. Most options brokers charge a margin requirement only for one side of the iron condor. The reasoning is that the trader should be right on one side or the other of this trade, so the maximum loss for the iron condor position is limited to the maximum loss for one of the credit spreads. So the iron condor has a margin requirement whereas the debit condor does not, and this brings us to the subject of the next section: Why trade the iron condor over a debit condor?

The Debit Condor vs. The Iron Condor

Consider the example position illustrated in Figure 13.2, the Russell 2000 Index (RUT) April iron condor with the RUT April 820/830 put spreads and the RUT April 980/990 call spreads. The price chart for the Russell 2000 Index is on the left of Figure 13.2 and one may run across horizontally from any price of RUT to the heavy black line, which is the profit and/or loss at expiration for this position. The position is profitable at expiration for any price of RUT between $828 and $982 (the light grey horizontal lines). This broad range of profitability is one of the attractive aspects of the iron condor spread. The red, blue and green lines on the risk/reward chart are the time decay curves giving us the value of the position between now and expiration. We will revisit this example as we discuss various aspects of the iron condor spread. But notice a couple of important characteristics of this trade set-up. First of all, we will enjoy a significant gain of 18%, and it will occur over a rather wide price range of RUT, over $154 wide! The break-evens for this iron condor are well outside of plus and minus one standard deviation; therefore, the probabilities of success for this position are on the order of 85-90%. But don't forget the downside risk. Assuming that we sold ten contracts for a net credit of $1,550 (our maximum gain), we could possibly lose as much as $8,450. The probabilities of that happening are small, probably of the order of 10-15%, but if the loss occurs, it would be catastrophic, wiping out several months of gains.

Imagine that the trader sets up an iron condor on RUT every month through the year and positions the spreads similarly to what we did in Figure 13.2. Based on the probabilities of success, we could reasonably expect the full profit of $1,550 about 10 months out of the year. This results a total gain of $15,550. But that also means that we might reasonably expect to take the full loss of $8,450 in 2 separate months for a total loss of $16,900. Thus, at the end of the year our account is underwater by about fourteen hundred dollars, or more when you also include the costs of trading commissions. This result is not unusual; review Chapter 2 and the discussions of probability distributions for the details. Options are priced based on their underlying probabilities of expiring in the money. Therefore, in order to achieve profitability in the long term, a system of trade management must be employed to ensure that we never incur the maximum loss. Later in this chapter, we will discuss various techniques for controlling the risk while trading the iron condor spread. For now, keep in mind this essential truth: a system of robust risk management is essential for long-term profitability while trading the iron condor. In the iron condor illustrated in Figure 13.2, we used two credit spreads. But we may also create a debit condor spread using all call options or all put options, as we saw earlier in this chapter. The debit condors built either with all call options or all put options will have virtually identical maximum profits and maximum losses. If we compare these debit condors to the iron condor at the same strike prices, we will again find similar risk/reward ratios. This is an example of a principle of the basic vertical spread extended to the multi-legged condor spread, viz., the maximum gain and the maximum loss of the vertical spread created with calls or the vertical spread created with puts at the same strike prices will always be virtually identical. The returns for the GOOGL 600/610 bull call spread and the GOOGL 600/610 bull put spread will be the same. We are seeing the same principle at work when we compare the iron condor with a condor created with all calls or all puts, i.e., the debit condors. So why do some people prefer the iron condor to a debit condor?

There are two principal advantages to the iron condor that I personally find persuasive. First is the opportunity to allow one or both of the spreads to enter expiration and expire worthless. I save not only the trading commissions, but also the net debit required to close the spreads. That debit may be small, i.e., $0.20 or less, but that is $20 per spread and may add up to a significant amount of money, depending on the volume of contracts you are trading. Traders often underestimate the significance of these potential savings.

Consider this hypothetical example: I am trading twenty contracts in my iron condor positions each month and paying $0.50 per contract in trading commissions. Let's assume that I can allow the spreads on one side or the other of my iron condor to expire worthless six months out of the year. We will also assume that if I had closed those spreads early rather than letting them expire, I would have had to pay $0.20 to close them. In this hypothetical situation, my total savings by allowing the spreads to expire worthless would have been about $2,500 over the period of one year. So having the opportunity to achieve the full profit on one or both of the credit spreads in my iron condor from time to time can add significantly to my long-term profitability.

The second advantage is available when one is trading larger numbers of contracts with the iron condor. Most brokers sweep the cash in one's account into money market funds on a daily basis and that interest may be significant on the credits received from larger positions and this will increase one's returns over time. Today's interest rates are near zero, so this isn't the advantage it has been in the past, but interest rates will be higher in the future.

So the differences in a debit condor and an iron condor are relatively small, but the ability to allow spreads to expire worthless and the interest earned on the credit received will boost one's returns with the iron condor over the long term.

My Condor May Not Be Your Condor

The condor options spread is a very versatile position. It may be configured in several different ways. These different configurations will result in higher or lower probabilities of success, larger or smaller risk/reward ratios, and widely varying levels of profitability. We addressed the differences between the iron condor and the debit condor above. The primary advantage of the iron condor is the ability to allow far OTM spreads to expire worthless as we enter expiration; this saves some expenses and increases our profitability.

If we position our iron condor spreads in closer (less OTM), we create an iron condor with a lower probability of success and a smaller risk/reward ratio. Often this position is created with about thirty days to expiration to maximize the rate of time decay. This condor will have a larger maximum rate of return, but the position needs to be managed closely. The position's profit or loss will fluctuate quickly with changes in the price of the underlying index. On the other hand, you may not be in this position for very long; this form of the iron condor can often be closed for a profit within two weeks. I have reduced some of my risk by being in the trade for less time and thereby minimizing my exposure to unexpected economic or global events that may move the market.

The polar opposite of this short-term iron condor is the condor positioned with its spreads far OTM at two to three months from expiration. Since the spreads are farther OTM, the credits received are smaller and thus the maximum rates of return are smaller. But the market moves are not as likely to cause rapid fluctuations in the position's profit or loss. Since the credits are smaller, one is forced to carry this condor position much closer to expiration to lock in as much of the initial credit as possible. Some traders prefer this condor because it does move slower and is therefore less stressful for the trader. However, all condor positions require close monitoring and adjustment to be successful. One disadvantage of this longer-term iron condor is that I am exposed to the market and global events far longer; that translates to increased risk.

Iron condors are commonly configured with ten dollar spread widths on the Standard and Poors 500 Index (SPX) and the Russell 2000 index (RUT), and twenty five dollar widths on the NASDAQ 100 Index (NDX). The twenty-five dollar widths for NDX are inherent in the options offered for NDX – they are commonly only available at twenty-five dollar strikes. The effects of the varying spread widths are illustrated in Table 13.1 where I have configured iron condor spreads on SPX, RUT and NDX, using different spread widths. The two condors with RUT are using ten dollar and twenty dollar spreads.

Table 13.1
The Effect of Spread Width

Index	Spreads	Max. Gain	Max. Loss	Probability	Number for Max Risk $5k
RUT	730/740 870/880	$172	$828	87%	6
RUT	720/740 870/890	$297	$1703	87%	3
SPX	1290/1300 1490/1500	$168	$832	88%	6
SPX	1280/1300 1480/1500	$305	$1695	88%	3
NDX	2375/2400 2875/2900	$295	$2205	93%	2

The SPX condors are also configured with ten and twenty dollar spreads and a twenty-five dollar spread is used for NDX. The maximum gain and loss for each condor is computed for one contract positions. The probability of the index expiring at expiration between the two short strikes is shown for each condor position. It is interesting that the probability of success for these trades is essentially the same for all configurations, but the maximum loss varies widely. In general, as I make my condor spread wider, I am increasing the profitability in absolute dollar terms, because the long option positioned farther OTM is less expensive, so the credit received is larger. But I am also widening the spread, which means the maximum potential loss is larger; the net effect is a decrease in the return on capital at risk. For example, the return for the ten-dollar RUT condor is 21%, but that return decreases to 17% when the spread width increases to twenty dollars.

The long option in each spread is effectively the hedge for that spread and serves to limit the loss on that side. Placing that option farther OTM costs less and therefore increases the credit received for the spread. But that wider spread significantly increases the downside risk. As we see in these examples, the downside risk roughly doubles as we double the spread width. Some condor traders use a wider spread to increase the absolute income generated by the position, but the return on investment is lower due to the increased capital at risk. The increased downside risk must be addressed either by trading fewer contracts or by modifying one's risk management rules to be more aggressive about making adjustments earlier when the index moves against the position.

The last column in Table 13.1 lists the number of contracts we could use for each of these condors if our money management rules limit us to a maximum loss of $5,000 on any single position. In each case, I have simply divided the maximum loss into $5,000 to determine the number of contracts to trade. However, many condor traders will use their experience with their risk management rules to set what they consider to be the largest likely loss, given their risk management system. If a trader has been trading RUT iron condors with ten dollar spreads for the past 2-3 years, she has sufficient experience to estimate her likely maximum loss in practice as a smaller number than the absolute maximum theoretical loss. Many experienced iron condor traders estimate the maximum loss on a given trade as approximately one to two months of gains.

This discussion brings us to a slightly different question that students often ask. If a trader has decided to trade long-term iron condors on RUT, is there an optimal spread width that should be used?

Table 13.2
Optimal Spread Width For RUT

Spread Width	Put Spreads	Call Spreads	#Cts	Credit	Max. Loss	Max. Return	R/R Ratio
$5	815/820	930/935	10	$1020	$3980	26%	3.90
$5	815/820	930/935	20	$2040	$7960	26%	3.90
$10	810/820	930/940	10	$1870	$8130	23%	4.35
$20	800/820	930/950	10	$3170	$16830	19%	5.31
$20	800/820	930/950	5	$1585	$8415	19%	5.31

Table 13.2 was developed on 1/4/13 with RUT trading at $879. I have set the short strikes at the same position in every one of these iron condor spreads. Notice that the risk/reward ratio is constant as I vary the number of contracts at a particular spread width but increases as the spread width increases. For an equal number of contracts, the credit received increases as the spread width increases. But the maximum loss is also increasing and thus the maximum return on capital at risk is decreasing. Therefore, we have an increasing risk/reward ratio with increasing spread width due to the increasing maximum loss.

In Chapter 2 we saw that an increasing probability of success accompanies an increasing risk/reward ratio. Thus, high probability trades always have large risk/reward ratios. In Table 13.2, we have a slightly different situation. The short strike price is identical for each of these spreads, yet we observe the risk/reward ratio increasing as the spread width increases. The probabilities of these spreads on RUT closing OTM at expiration for the maximum gain are identical. The probabilities of these spreads closing completely ITM at expiration for the maximum loss are actually decreasing as the spread width increases. However, the probability of RUT closing somewhere within the spread is increasing. Thus, in Table 13.2, we see an increasing risk/reward ratio as the maximum loss increases, even though the probability of success is constant.

If I adjust the number of contracts to hold the maximum loss, or risk, constant, then we see that the maximum return decreases as the spread width increases. This should drive the trader to favor five-dollar spreads for his iron condor over ten or twenty dollar spreads. However, in practice, if one is trading far OTM spreads in a long-term iron condor on RUT, he may find that only ten-dollar spreads are available at the strike prices desired. But more and more strikes are being offered over time, so this may be a diminishing issue. Another issue constraining the strike price selection is open interest. Five dollar spreads have been offered on SPX and RUT for some time, but the open interest may be very small at the five dollar strikes, e.g., lower at $1985 and higher at $1980 and $1990.

Another variation on the theme of the iron condor is to position the spreads far OTM and three to six months out in time. The objective of this trade is to allow time decay to create small profits in one or both spreads over the first 30 to 60 days of the trade and then close the position well in advance of expiration.

One of the advantages of the iron condor is its flexibility and the wide variety of configurations. This naturally leads us to the question posed in the next section.

The Best Iron Condor Strategy

Novice traders often presume there is a "best" way to trade the iron condor, but that isn't true. In this chapter, we have discussed several different variations on the iron condor; and this has not been an exhaustive review. You may hear or read someone cite a "rule" for trading the iron condor, such as:

➢ Close either spread when you achieve 50% of the maximum gain.

Remember that many, if not all, of the rules proposed for trading the iron condor are dependent on the configuration of the iron condor preferred by that trader. It may or may not be applicable to your trading system. For example, the 50% profit stop cited above is commonly used for short-term iron condors placed closer to the current value of the underlying index. When the trader has collected a premium of two dollars, closing the spread for a one dollar gain makes sense. However, if the original credit received was only fifty cents for a long-term far OTM iron condor, that 50% profit stop would not be optimal.

I have also frequently heard and read the following rule for trading the iron condor:

> Initiate the iron condor position when implied volatility is high.

If a directional trader is using the iron condor in conjunction with his predictions about the market's direction and volatility, then this rule makes sense. The iron condor spread is a negative vega position, so declining implied volatility favors the position. Some traders like to sell the iron condor just before an earnings announcement to take advantage of the declining implied volatility after the announcement. But that is an aggressive trade; the trader will either profit or lose money overnight – the classic binary trade.

However, the non-directional trader isn't predicting price direction or volatility changes. He uses a standard deviation calculation each month to position the spreads in the condor to incur consistent levels of risk. The level of implied volatility is incorporated into the standard deviation calculation. Thus, the spreads will be positioned farther OTM when implied volatility is high and less far OTM when implied volatility contracts.

This rule of selling iron condor spreads when implied volatility is high most commonly comes from a trader who positions the condor spreads at a fixed dollar amount from the current index price. When implied volatility is high, he is receiving a larger credit for his spreads, but may not realize that he is actually positioning his spreads at lower probabilities of success, i.e., the probability of the underlying stock or index price hitting either of the short strikes of his spreads is higher when implied volatility is higher.

Again, this isn't about "right or wrong". Many different ways of trading the iron condor exist, but my trading system may not be your trading system. Beware of self-proclaimed gurus and their pronouncements of the "right way" to trade the iron condor.

Stocks, Indexes or ETFs?

Another variation on the condor theme is the choice of the underlying: stock or index? Our focus in this book is on non-directional trading. If I am following a particular stock and I am predicting a sideways trading pattern for the immediate future, then using an iron condor to profit from that prediction is a good choice. But that would be a directional trade based on my prediction of price and time.

If I am trading non-directionally, I am diligently not making any predictions about the future. I am simply using a set of rules to respond to today's market moves. This trading philosophy is normally used for monthly income generation. Since I wish to minimize the price moves that might require me to adjust the position, I prefer using a broad index option for these iron condor positions, e.g., SPX, RUT, NDX, etc. These indexes are based on a large number of stocks and therefore, the index price will be less volatile than any single stock price.

Table 13.3
Index vs. ETF

Index or ETF	Put Spreads	Call Spreads	Number of Contracts	Credit Received	Max. Loss	Max. Return
SPX	1390/1400	1520/1530	10	$2420	$7580	32%
SPY	139/140	152/153	10	$250	$750	33%
RUT	800/810	930/940	10	$1520	$8480	18%
IWM	80/81	93/94	10	$160	$840	19%

Many of these broad-based index options have a corresponding Exchange Traded Fund or ETF. For example, the ETF corresponding to SPX is SPY, and similarly, the ETF for RUT is IWM. Each of these ETFs has options, so one could create an iron condor position on SPY or IWM. But the scale of the ETFs is different from the indexes. For example, SPY is one tenth of SPX. See the examples I have created in Table 13.3. These iron condors were established on 1/7/13 with ten contracts at approximately plus and minus one standard deviation with the February options (38 days to expiration) while SPX was trading at $1459 and RUT was trading at $874.

The scale difference between these indexes and their corresponding ETFs is obvious from Table 13.3. The iron condor positioned in approximately the same relative positions in SPY and IWM brings in a credit that is about 10% of the credit received in the iron condors placed on the indexes, SPX and RUT. Therefore, trading the index or the ETF is equivalent in terms of profitability and the risk/reward ratio. The difference is scale. If I have a $20,000 account, I may wish to trade the ten contract iron condor on SPX so as to leave myself extra capital to adjust and manage the position. To generate the same potential gains in this account with iron condors on SPY, I would trade 100 contracts, and therefore would be incurring much larger trading commission expenses. The advantage of using ETF options for the iron condor is for smaller accounts. If and when the trader scales up his position size, he would be well advised to move to the corresponding index options to lessen the impact of trading commissions.

Sometimes my students ask about using ETF options to hedge their iron condors built with index options. From the scale differences you see in Table 13.3, it is apparent why this isn't practical. One would require ten times as many contracts in the ETF options to achieve the same hedging effect as would be achieved with one index option. However, if one had a smaller iron condor position built with RUT options, e.g., 5 contracts, hedging that position with 2-3 IWM options might be a more optimal hedge. In that situation, hedging with a RUT option would be overwhelming.

Condor Safety Nets

In the next section, we will discuss a variety of techniques used to manage and adjust the iron condor position. But all iron condor positions should be protected with what I call the *safety net*. Think of this as analogous to the trapeze artists in the circus. They probably don't think they need the safety net, but, just in case…

The simplest safety net is an order to close the put spreads if the underlying index trades below a certain price. Most brokers refer to this as a contingent order that will be sent to the floor automatically if the trigger for the contingency is met. Markets always drop much faster than they rise, so I only use the contingency stop loss order on the put spreads in my iron condor.

The trader may add to his safety net by buying one or more long-term ATM puts. We buy a put about six months out in time because the time decay (theta) is less; thus, our daily cost for this insurance is lower. We would roll this put up or down as time goes on, either taking a loss or booking a gain. But, on average, this insurance costs us some of our gains each month. In the event of a sudden downdraft in the market, volatility will spike; our put will dramatically appreciate in price due to the actual price move (the delta effect) coupled with the volatility effect (the vega effect). When coupled with a contingency closing order, the trader awakes to the market disaster with his put spreads closed and a long put position that is building large gains by the minute. This may not prevent a loss, but it will significantly mitigate the loss.

How many puts should I buy? Calculating the optimal hedging positions for a portfolio isn't a trivial proposition. For the reader who is interested in the details, I suggest Larry McMillan's classic, *Options As A Strategic Investment*. McMillan's audience includes institutional managers with large and varied portfolios. The audience of this book is the retail trader (people like me). For our purposes, we can approximate the number of puts in the following way. Use an option calculator from your broker's web site to estimate the value of an ATM put on the index being traded, assuming that the volatility remains constant and the index price drops to the short put strike price. This gives you the delta effect of this move on the put. Then add in a large volatility spike of at least a 50% rise.

That will give the trader a rough estimate of the gains for that single ATM put in the event of a market crash. Estimate the losses on your put spreads if the contingency order triggers. With this information, the trader can estimate the number of puts to purchase for the number of contracts in the iron condor position. I have estimated that one ATM put should be an adequate hedge for every twenty contracts in the iron condor position. I haven't traded the iron condor through a catastrophic market crash such as that of October 1987, but the more severe the crash, the larger the volatility spike, and thus, the protection of the ATM put would be amplified.

Trade Management And Adjustment

The iron condor may be configured in several different ways, resulting in positions with widely varying risk/reward ratios and probabilities of success. It is relatively easy to enter the iron condor trade, and, if you are fortunate, you may make some reasonable profits the first few times you use this trade. But sooner or later, the market will move against the position, and the novice trader will find himself giving back most or all of his gains.

In 2011, many iron condor traders made excellent profits until the crash in August. Many of those traders ended 2011 "in the red" – they lost everything they gained earlier in the year. We demonstrated earlier that our only chance at long-term profitability trading the iron condor is via a robust risk management system. The word, system, implies a well-defined set of rules for entry, exit and adjusting the iron condor. Describing this as a robust system means we have performed our due diligence to assure ourselves that this system of risk management rules actually works in the real world. We have back-tested the rules, and we have experimented with small positions before scaling up to larger numbers of contracts.

As the market index moves up or down and begins to pressure one side of our condor position, we need to be able to hedge or adjust the position. Some adjustment techniques minimize the position's downside risk by closing a portion or all of the spreads. Other adjustments hedge the position, minimizing our losses and allowing us to remain in the position a bit longer to allow time for the market to pull back. If the market does not pull back, then our adjustment minimized the loss taken when the position was eventually closed.

This raises a crucial point that is often misunderstood. Adjustment strategies for the iron condor do not assure the trader of never taking a loss. That is an unrealistic expectation. Options traders of all stripes will take losses — that is the overhead cost of this business. Risk management has the objective of minimizing losses when they occur so that long-term profitability is assured. Every iron condor position has the potential of taking a loss that could wipe out several months of condor profits. The trader's risk management system must eliminate that possibility and reduce losses to something manageable, i.e., losing one or two months of previous gains as a worst case.

Entering the iron condor position is relatively easy. Managing the trade is the tricky part.

Several different adjustments for the iron condor are feasible; the following summary of adjustment techniques is not an exhaustive list. Each of these adjustments has its own advantages and disadvantages. Some adjustment techniques are best in specific market environments. A particular condor adjustment technique will not be the best adjustment in every circumstance.

The 200% Rule

The most conservative and simplest technique for controlling the risk of the iron condor is the 200% rule. The trader watches each spread in the condor and monitors the debit required to close the spread. Whenever the debit to close the spread is double the original credit received for that spread, the 200% rule is triggered and we close the spreads on that side of the condor. Since the credits received on each side of the condor are typically similar in magnitude, the 200% rule normally results in a small loss, break-even, or a small gain.

When you look at the condor position on your brokers screen, remember that you will be able to negotiate to close the trade for less than the ask price. So don't trigger the 200% rule based on the ask price. When the ask price to close the spread exceeds the 200% price, that is our "red flag" to be on alert; we may have to exercise the 200% rule shortly.

The beauty of the 200% rule is simplicity. Novice traders can use the 200% rule and avoid the large losses that are unfortunately all too common for beginners. The power of the 200% rule is that it stops out trade positions early and avoids the large losses that may occur. Ironically, the disadvantage of the 200% rule is essentially the same trait, viz., it frequently stops out our positions. I have often had beginning students trade the iron condor using the 200% rule and achieve profitability in their first year. But in volatile market environments, the 200% rule will result in many trades being stopped out early.

Closing Spreads

Another very simple way of managing one's risk with the iron condor is to close a portion of the spreads that are under pressure. For example, if the index price has moved up significantly and our call spreads are losing money, we could close a portion of those call spreads to reduce our downside risk. Traders normally trigger this adjustment by the index price crossing a price threshold or by tracking the delta value of the short option in the spread.

I will illustrate with a couple of examples. In the first example, the call spreads of our condor on the Russell 2000 Index (RUT) are positioned at 910/920 with RUT trading at $877. The trigger for our adjustment is when RUT trades above $893, the halfway point between the starting price of the underlying index and the short strike price of the call spread. Then we close one third of the call spreads in our condor. When RUT trades above $902, three quarters of the distance to the short strike, we close the remaining call spreads.

Using the same RUT iron condor with call spreads positioned at 910/920, we may trigger our adjustment based on the delta of the short strike in the spread under pressure. When the delta of the 910 call option hits 16, we close one third of the call spreads in our condor. If, at a later time, the delta of the 910 call option hits 25, we would close the remaining call spreads.

Either method of triggering the adjustment is equally valid and effective. The trader should also configure the adjustment trigger based on his risk tolerance profile. A more risk averse trader should trigger the adjustments earlier, either with a closer price or a smaller delta value.

Conversely, the more aggressive trader might use a price trigger or a delta value that allows the index to move farther against the position before triggering the adjustment.

Closing spreads is another reasonably conservative and simple way to manage the risk of the iron condor spread. If the index price trends against our position, this adjustment will minimize the loss incurred.

The Long Hedge

The long hedge adjustment is created by buying one or more long options in the next expiration month. Similar to the adjustments above, the long hedge may be triggered by either the value of the underlying index, the delta of the short option, or the overall position delta. I recommend using the delta of the short option in the spread as the adjustment trigger for this adjustment. When the adjustment triggers, the trader goes out to the next expiration month and buys one or more long options at the strike price of the short options in the iron condor spread under pressure. As the index continues to move against the position, the long hedge options are mitigating the losses of the iron condor. If the index pulls back, the trader would sell the long hedge options.

Consider this example, an iron condor on the Russell 2000 Index (RUT) with the February call spreads positioned at 910/920 and RUT trading at $877. A week after we have entered this position, RUT has traded upward and the delta of the 910 call is now 19. This triggers the long hedge adjustment and we buy one 910 call option in the March expiration month. Now we have a hedged position; if RUT continues upward, the March 910 call option will continue to appreciate in value, somewhat offsetting the losses in the February 910/920 call spreads. If RUT trades sideways or pulls back so that the delta of the February 910 call drops below 17, we then would sell the March 910 call.

My general rule it is to buy the hedge option in the next month at the short strike of the spread in the condor that is under pressure. However, I always model several possible adjustments, using different strike prices and also different numbers of hedge options. But the starting place for my long hedge adjustment is to use the short strike price of the spread under pressure in the iron condor and buy one hedge option for every ten current condor spreads.

The principal advantage of the long hedge adjustment is the fact that we salvage our condor spread and much of our potential profit in the event the index moves against us but then pulls back or trades sideways. Be careful not to remove the hedge option too quickly; if, for example, RUT had pulled back such that the delta of the short option was now 19, our trigger value, don't remove the hedge option. If you remove the hedge option too early you are exposed to a possible whipsaw in the index price. Leaving the hedge option in place for a little longer does cost you some of your profit, but it minimizes your risk in volatile markets. It is important to realize that our adjustments have a price. This is analogous to buying insurance on my house. At the end of the year, my house has not burned down, but I still had to pay my insurance premium.

One can think of the long hedge adjustment process for the iron condor as consisting of three steps:

1. The first trigger point is reached and we employ the long hedge adjustment, i.e., buying a long hedge option in the next month.
2. The second trigger point is reached as the index continues its move against the position, and the spreads on that side of the condor are closed.
3. The third step can go in one of two directions. More conservative and less experienced traders should simply close any long options left from the long hedge adjustments, allow the other spreads to expire worthless and the trade is over. More experienced traders may consider leaving any long hedge options in place and rolling the spreads up or down, e.g., if the index was moving down against our put spreads, we close the original put spreads and open new put spreads farther OTM.

It is worth noting that the condor trader utilizing the long hedge form of adjustment will find that this technique works better in falling markets than rising markets. When the market is trending upward, implied volatility is falling. This effect causes our hedge call options to not appreciate as rapidly as the market advances against our condor position. But when the market drops, implied volatility spikes upward and the hedge put options appreciate dramatically. My iron condor positions have suffered lesser losses when the market was trending downward because of this volatility effect.

Other Adjustments

There are several other adjustment techniques that I have chosen not to address in detail. One is the Buy Back adjustment, where our adjustment triggers a closing of one or more of the short options in the spread under pressure. This adjustment suffers a serious disadvantage: it reduces our position theta to a large degree because we are closing the short options in the spread that are generating that positive theta.

Another possible condor adjustment is to create a butterfly spread out of the credit spread that is under pressure from the advancing index. The resulting butterfly spread is a powerful hedge for the iron condor position under pressure, but I don't use this adjustment primarily because it requires the trader to put significantly more capital at risk in the trade.

Before we leave this discussion of adjustment techniques, I should emphasize one point lest it be misunderstood. Choose your preferred adjustment technique before you establish the iron condor position. Write all of the rules associated with this adjustment in your trading journal. Don't mix adjustment techniques while in the midst of the trade.

Rolling Spreads

Whenever my adjustment has triggered, but the index has continued to move against my position, I am forced to close the spreads on that side of the iron condor position. My choices are:

1. Close the spreads and close the long hedge options. Allow the spreads on the other side to expire worthless.
2. Close the spreads and leave the long hedge options open. Open new spreads farther OTM and continue the trade.

Rolling spreads are only recommended for iron condor traders with at least two years experience with this trade. To illustrate the trade-offs, consider a hypothetical example of rolling spreads.

The initial position is established by selling 20 call spreads for $0.90, and 20 put spreads for $1.00, thus a total credit of $3,800. The index moves up and triggers my adjustment with the delta of the short call reaching 18; I hedge with two calls in the next month out for a total debit of $1,800.

The index continues to move up, and I close the original call spreads for $3.20 for a debit of $6,400 (20 x 320). I roll up and open new call spreads; the index slows and I close the hedges for a net gain of $1,100. My put spreads expire worthless for a gain of $2,000. Therefore, before I look at the results of the rolled call spreads, I have a net loss of $1500 (initial credit of $3,800 plus a gain of $1,100 on the hedge options, less the $6,400 for closing the call spreads).

We had several choices for the roll, but these scenarios will give you a sense of the trade-offs involved.

1) I could have rolled up just one or two strikes and sold new spreads for $1.85, thus receiving a credit of $3,700. I then closed the calls before expiration for $0.50 or a debit of $1,000. Thus, I could have a net gain of $2,700 on the calls and a net gain of $1,200 for the entire position.

2) Another possibility would have been to roll the new call spreads out to one standard deviation OTM and collect a credit of $0.70 or $1,400. If I closed the calls before expiration for $0.20 or a debit of $400, I would have had a net gain of $1,000 on the calls and a net loss on the iron condor of $500.

3) The third possible adjustment would be to open a larger number of contracts on the roll. If I had sold 30 contracts of the new call spreads at one standard deviation OTM, I would have collected a credit of $0.70 or $2,100. I then could have closed the calls before expiration for $0.20 or a debit of $600, leaving me with a net gain of $1,500 on the calls and a net gain on the entire position of $500.

We have several choices when deciding to close and roll spreads in an iron condor position. When I roll the spreads only by a couple of strikes, I collect a larger credit that serves to salvage more of the cost of closing the original spreads. But the risk is that the index continues to move against me and I have to close and roll again. I will almost certainly have a net loss after incurring the cost of closing losing spreads twice.

If I choose to roll the spreads farther OTM, it is a safer move, but I collect a smaller credit and this move probably brings the position roughly to break-even or a small loss.

If I roll farther OTM, but also increase the number of contracts, I can probably turn the condor into a profitable play. But the trade-off is that I have increased the risk (and the margin) on that side of the condor.

As this example demonstrates, rolling spreads with iron condors can be dangerous work. Several judgment calls are required and one may incur an even larger loss in the process of closing and rolling spreads. Don't roll spreads if you are a novice or a conservative iron condor trader. There is nothing wrong with being conservative.

This discussion has focused on rolling the spreads that are under pressure from the advancing index. What if my spreads on one side or the other are far OTM and may be closed for $0.10? If you have several weeks before expiration, you will be tempted to close and roll those spreads more ITM to boost the gains of the position. This can be very tempting because it could easily increase the returns from that month's condor by 50% or more.

But don't forget the additional risk that is being accepted by that roll. I have had the experience of rolling those spreads up or down and then having the index reverse course on me. Then I find myself hustling to hedge this side of the condor that was quite safe just a few days earlier. As a result, I am cautious about rolling spreads to increase the gains on a position.

When rolling the spreads on the profitable side of the iron condor position, I position the new spreads more conservatively than I did for the initial position. For example, I may have collected an initial credit of $0.75 for the put spreads and the market has now traded upward, allowing me to close the put spreads for $0.10 with three weeks remaining until expiration. I will position the new put spreads far enough out of the money that I may only collect a credit of $0.45, much less than I would accept initially. I have boosted my profitability on this position, but have carefully controlled the additional risk.

Volatility And The Iron Condor

Condor and iron condor spreads are negative vega positions, i.e., increasing implied volatility decreases the value of the position while decreasing implied volatility increases the value of the position. In Chapter 9 we discussed the vega risk of the calendar spread, but the risk is the opposite for the calendar spread: increasing implied volatility helps the calendar while decreasing implied volatility hurts its profitability.

Recall the discussion of the effects of implied volatility changes on the vertical spread in Chapter 7. Increased implied volatility does not change the profitability of the vertical spread at expiration, but it does make it harder to close the trade early. And the condor and iron condor both consist of two vertical spreads so it is precisely the same situation. When implied volatility increases, it shifts the current risk/reward curves out away from the risk/reward curve at expiration. Thus, at a given index price and time to expiration, the gain that could be realized by closing the spread early has been diminished. Or, if the condor stands at a net loss, closing early when implied volatility has risen will result in a larger loss.

The vega risk of the condor presents itself commonly in just this way: the index plummets and the condor is losing value simply on the basis of the price drop, but implied volatility is also rising as the market drops, so our position is also losing value due to increased implied volatility. Our position is taking a double hit.

But if the index pulls back or trades sideways to close at expiration within the channel of our condor, then we achieve the maximum profit displayed by the risk/reward curve at expiration. So the vega risk is very real and measurable, but it applies to us only if we are forced to close our spread early. The ultimate profitability computed for the condor initially is unchanged by changes in implied volatility.

A related question is this: should we favor establishing our condor when implied volatility is high so we can receive larger credits and improve our returns? For the non-directional trader, the answer is no. Allow me to explain.

A trader commonly establishes the iron condor in one of three ways. He may calculate one standard deviation and place the spreads with reference to that price, or he may consistently sell the option with a particular delta value, e.g., he looks through the calls and the puts for the strike prices where delta ≈ 10. Other traders may choose the spread farthest OTM where they can still receive a minimum credit, e.g., $0.85. It may not be obvious at first blush, but all of these methods of positioning the spreads have included the effects of implied volatility.

Increased implied volatility is effectively self-correcting for the non-directional iron condor trader. When implied volatility is high, the prices of the individual options are higher and the credits received will be larger. If I position my spreads based on a minimum credit, I will observe that my spreads will be farther OTM when implied volatility is higher. But that doesn't mean the position is safer because increased implied volatility tells us the market is expecting wider swings in price in the near future.

If I position my spreads with a standard deviation calculation, then the increased implied volatility is taken into account by that calculation and this results in a larger standard deviation. Then the spreads are positioned farther OTM. Again, the increased implied volatility was accommodated automatically by the standard deviation calculation.

If we think of delta as an estimate of the probability of the option expiring ITM, then it makes sense that higher implied volatility would correspond with higher deltas for the individual options. As implied volatility increases, the probability of any particular option expiring ITM has also increased. Hence the trader who positions his iron condor spreads based on the delta of the short option has already incorporated increased implied volatility into the positioning of his spreads.

Therefore, the non-directional condor trader is indifferent to the levels of implied volatility when establishing his position. However, if implied volatility is increasing as the index threatens one side of the trader's condor, the profit and loss position will be damaged by both the price move of the index and the negative vega of the condor. But the ultimate profitability of the condor at expiration is unchanged by the increased implied volatility.

Confusion has arisen over this question of placing iron condors when implied volatility is high because of a misunderstanding of the distinction of the directional versus the non-directional trader. If I am using an iron condor position as a result of my predictions for the future price movement and volatility of the underlying stock or index, then selling the iron condor in a time of high volatility with the expectation of declining volatility makes sense. But the non-directional trader is trading the iron condor each month without making any predictions of future price or volatility movement. This trader positions her spreads based on a standard deviation calculation, so the effects of implied volatility are already included. Higher levels of implied volatility result in larger values of the standard deviation and therefore, the spreads are positioned farther OTM, compensating for the higher risk implied by higher volatility.

On the other hand, the directional trader may only sell his iron condor positions a few times per year because he is waiting for higher levels of implied volatility. He may always position his spreads along a preset channel of price, e.g., plus or minus $100 on the SPX. When implied volatility is high, those spreads return larger credits. As volatility declines, the iron condor position will appreciate in value. This trader may not realize that his probability of success is lower for these positions. The non-directional iron condor trader is striving to establish positions with consistent levels of high probability of success. Put another way, the non-directional iron condor trader wants to not only minimize his risk from month to month, but also incur a consistent level of risk from month to month.

Back Testing The Iron Condor Trading Systems

In Chapter 11, we back tested several possible trading systems for the butterfly spread used as a non-directional income generation trade. Refer back to that discussion to remind yourself of the limitations of back testing. Back testing is a valuable tool for developing a trading system, but the limitations must always be considered.

I principally use two variations on the iron condor spread in my personal accounts. In the one, I initiate the trade at about 30 days to expiration, position the spreads in closer to the current price of the index, and use the 200% rule to manage the risk. I also trade the long-term iron condor, initiating the trade at 55-60 days to expiration, positioning the spreads well outside of one standard deviation OTM and use the long hedge to adjust the position. My detailed rules follow below; I trade SPX, RUT and NDX in my personal accounts, but used RUT for the back testing analysis.

Short Term Iron Condor Trading System

1. Establish the iron condor around 30 days to expiration on the Russell 2000 Index (RUT). Position the spreads inside of one standard deviation so that the delta of the short option in the spread has a value of approximately 17-20.
2. Enter the position one vertical spread at a time. Look at the one minute chart; if the market is trending upward intraday, enter the put spread order first. After that order is filled, enter the call spread order.
3. Enter a contingency stop loss order to trigger if the index trades below a value ten dollars above the short put option strike price.
4. Close all of the spreads on a side if the debit to close exceeds 200% of the original credit of that spread.
5. No profit stop is used.
6. Close all spreads on the Friday before expiration week.

Long Term Iron Condor Trading System

1. Establish the iron condor around 55-60 days to expiration on the Russell 2000 Index (RUT). Calculate one standard deviation (1σ) and position the spreads approximately 1.2 σ OTM (or with the delta of the short options at about 7-10).
2. Enter the position one vertical spread at a time. Look at the one minute chart; if the market is trending upward intraday, enter the put spread order first. After that order is filled, enter the call spread order.

3. Enter a contingency stop loss order. Position the trigger for this order at an index price where the delta of the short option in the put spreads is estimated to be about 35.
4. If the delta of the short option in either spread exceeds 18, buy an option at the same strike price one month out in time. Buy one hedge option for every ten condor spreads.
   a) If the index price pulls back and the delta of the short option drops below 16, sell the hedge options.
   b) If the index continues to move against the position and the delta of the short option reaches 30, close all of the spreads on that side and sell the hedge options.
5. No profit stop is used.
6. Compute one standard deviation (1σ) on the Friday before expiration week. Close either spread if the spread is less than 2σ OTM.

Figures 13.3 through 13.6 summarize the back testing results for these iron condor trading systems. Both condors were back tested on the Russell 2000 Index (RUT). The short-term iron condor back test assumed a beginning account size of $25,000 and twenty contracts of each condor were traded each month.

The results for back testing this short-term iron condor strategy were net gains of 73% in 2012 and 95% in 2013 (Figures 13.3 and 13.4). When one looks closer at the results, it is notable that over the two years or twenty-four trades, ten losses were incurred. This is a vivid demonstration of the power of a stop loss technique. Three of the losses were sizable: 19%, 19% and 28%, but the remaining three losses were ten percent or less. And two trades essentially broke even. So these very large gains were achieved with only twelve winners, or a 50% win/loss ratio. That is the power of the stop loss, in this case, the rather simple 200% rule.

Figure 13.3
Short-Term Iron Condor 2012 Back-Test Results

Expiration Month	Open Date	Spreads	Initial Credit	Close Date	Reason Closed	Net Return ($)	Net Return (%)	Portfolio Value	Portfolio Return (%)
Jan-12	12/20/11	660/670 790/800	$6,300	1/13/12	Time	$5,020	37%	$30,020	20.1%
Feb-12	1/17/12	700/710 810/820	$7,300	2/1/12	Stop Loss	-$2,440	-19%	$27,580	10.3%
Mar-12	2/14/12	750/760 860/870	$7,000	3/9/12	Time	$6,360	49%	$33,940	35.8%
Apr-12	3/20/12	770/780 870/880	$6,040	4/10/12	Stop Loss	$40	0%	$33,980	35.9%
May-12	4/17/12	750/760 850/860	$7,200	5/11/12	Time	$5,200	41%	$39,180	56.7%
Jun-12	5/15/12	710/720 820/830	$7,300	6/8/12	Time	$6,640	52%	$45,820	83.3%
Jul-12	6/19/12	720/730 820/830	$6,540	7/5/12	Stop Loss	-$2,500	-19%	$43,320	73.3%
Aug-12	7/17/12	740/750 840/850	$5,740	8/10/12	Time	$5,480	38%	$48,800	95.2%
Sep-12	8/21/12	760/770 850/860	$4,900	9/6/12	Stop Loss	-$500	-3%	$48,300	93.2%
Oct-12	9/18/12	810/820 890/900	$5,940	10/12/12	Stop Loss	-$360	-3%	$47,940	91.8%
Nov-12	10/16/12	780/790 870/880	$5,400	11/8/12	Stop Loss	-$1,200	-8%	$46,740	87.0%
Dec-12	11/20/12	750/760 820/830	$7,300	11/29/12	Stop Loss	-$3,540	-28%	$43,200	72.8%

Assumes a beginning balance of $25,000.
Trading commissions were not included.
Each iron condor consists of twenty RUT contracts.
Spreads were positioned at thirty days from expiration with delta of the short option at 17-20 .
No profit stop was used.
The 200% rule was used as the stop loss.
The time stop was the Friday before expiration week.

The results of back testing the long-term iron condor trading system outlined above are displayed in Figures 13.5 and 13.6 for 2012 and 2013. This back test assumed an account size of $50,000 with twenty contracts in each of the two iron condors open at any given time. For example, during the week following the expiration of the April options, the iron condor for June would be opened, so one would then have the May and June positions open. The advantage of this approach is spreading the portfolio risk over two months of time. The net portfolio returns were +47% with ten wins and two losses in 2012 and +29% in 2013 with nine wins and three losses.

Three positions in 2012 required adjustment using long hedge options in the following month; four positions were adjusted in 2013. In my experience, this frequency of adjustment was somewhat low. It is not unusual to adjust as many as nine out of twelve trades.

This trading system used the two sigma rule as the time stop, applied on the Friday before expiration week; this resulted in a closing of the spreads on one side of the position in three different months in 2012 and five times in 2013.

Figure 13.4
Short-Term Iron Condor 2013 Back-Test Results

Expiration Month	Open Date	Spreads	Initial Credit	Close Date	Reason Closed	Net Return ($)	Net Return (%)	Portfolio Value	Portfolio Return (%)
Jan-13	12/18/12	790/800 890/900	$4,240	1/2/13	Stop Loss	$0	0%	$25,000	0.0%
Feb-13	1/14/13	830/840 910/920	$6,100	1/25/13	Stop Loss	-$2,200	-10%	$22,800	-8.8%
Mar-13	2/12/13	870/880 950/960	$4,960	3/8/13	Time	$1,580	11%	$24,380	-2.5%
Apr-13	3/19/13	890/900 970/980	$7,000	4/12/13	Time	$6,460	50%	$30,840	23.4%
May-13	4/16/13	860/870 960/970	$5,600	4/30/13	Stop Loss	-$1,000	-5%	$29,840	19.4%
Jun-13	5/21/13	940/950 1040/1050	$5,080	6/7/13	Time	$2,260	15%	$32,100	28.4%
Jul-13	6/17/13	1110/1120 1220/1230	$5,960	7/12/13	Time	$5,460	39%	$37,560	50.2%
Aug-13	7/15/13	1090/1100 1200/1210	$6,500	8/9/13	Time	$5,860	43%	$43,420	73.7%
Sep-13	8/20/13	970/980 1070/1080	$6,400	9/13/13	Time	$3,240	24%	$46,660	86.6%
Oct-13	9/17/13	1000/1010 1110/1120	$5,800	10/11/13	Time	$3,980	28%	$50,640	102.6%
Nov-13	10/15/13	1010/1020 1130/1140	$6,200	10/29/13	Stop Loss	-$1,100	-5%	$49,540	98.2%
Dec-13	11/19/13	1040/1050 1140/1150	$6,300	11/25/13	Stop Loss	-$900	-4%	$48,640	94.6%

Assumes a beginning balance of $25,000.
Trading commissions were not included.
Each iron condor consists of twenty RUT contracts.
Spreads were positioned at thirty days from expiration with delta of the short option at 17-20.
No profit stop was used.
The 200% rule was used as the stop loss.
The time stop was the Friday before expiration week.

The contingency stop loss orders did not trigger in any of these back tests for the short-term or the long-term iron condor. In my experience, this is consistent with "real world" trading. The contingency stop loss will only be triggered in extreme market events where the trader did not have an opportunity to adjust the position and close spreads if necessary. But you will be thankful for that contingency stop loss order if something like the crash of 1987 occurs while you have positions open.

When a trader compares the results of these two trading systems, he might be tempted to immediately conclude that the short-term iron condor system is superior; after all, it achieved a much higher return in this back testing session over two years. But the higher return of the short-term system is accompanied by higher risk and more frequent trade management, i.e., adjusting and closing spreads. The trading style of these two systems is quite different. The short-term iron condor back test resulted in ten losses in twenty-four months whereas the long-term iron condor trading system had half as many losses during the testing period. Employing a trading system because it promises a higher return is not the right answer if it keeps you from sleeping at night.

Figure 13.5
Long-Term Iron Condor 2012 Back-Test Results

Expiration Month	Open Date	Spreads	Initial Credit	Adjustments	Two Sigma Close	Net Return ($)	Net Return (%)	Portfolio Value	Portfolio Return (%)
Jan-12	11/21/11	540/550 830/840	$3,940	0	no	$3,940	25%	$53,940	7.9%
Feb-12	12/20/11	600/610 840/850	$3,680	0	calls	$2,040	13%	$55,980	12.0%
Mar-12	1/25/12	660/670 870/880	$2,500	0	calls	$2,360	13%	$58,340	16.7%
Apr-12	2/22/12	670/680 900/910	$3,200	0	no	$3,200	19%	$61,540	23.1%
May-12	3/21/12	680/690 910/920	$2,860	0	no	$2,860	17%	$64,400	28.8%
Jun-12	4/25/12	680/690 880/890	$2,860	0	no	$2,860	17%	$67,260	34.5%
Jul-12	5/23/12	630/640 850/860	$3,460	0	calls	$3,460	21%	$70,720	41.4%
Aug-12	6/20/12	660/670 860/870	$3,240	1	no	$2,680	16%	$73,400	46.8%
Sep-12	7/25/12	650/660 850/860	$2,900	2	no	-$3,690	-22%	$69,710	39.4%
Oct-12	8/22/12	690/700 880/890	$2,800	1	no	-$2,310	-13%	$67,400	34.8%
Nov-12	9/26/12	710/720 900/910	$2,560	0	no	$2,560	15%	$69,960	39.9%
Dec-12	10/24/12	700/710 880/890	$3,400	0	no	$3,400	20%	$73,360	46.7%

Assumes a beginning balance of $50,000.
Trading commissions were not included.
Each iron condor consists of twenty RUT contracts; at any given time, two positions are open.
Condors were initiated the week following option expiration at about 55-60 days to expiration.
Spreads were positioned with delta of the short option from 7-10.
No profit stop was used.
The long hedge was used when delta of the short option > 18.
If delta of the short option > 30, spreads and the hedge options were closed.
The time stop used the two sigma rule on the Friday before expiration week.

Comparing the back testing results of the short-term and long-term iron condors illustrates a common principle of options trading. Trades with higher potential profitability always display a wider range of results, i.e., larger gains accompanied by larger losses. The short-term iron condor back testing resulted in much larger overall gains than the long-term iron condor. The monthly results for the short-term condor trading system ranged from a loss of 28% to a gain of 52%, whereas the results for the long-term condor ranged from a loss of 22% to a gain of 25%. This larger volatility of the short-term condor results is typical of trading systems with high potential returns.

Figure 13.6
Long-Term Iron Condor 2013 Back-Test Results

Expiration Month	Open Date	Spreads	Initial Credit	Adjustments	Two Sigma Close	Net Return ($)	Net Return (%)	Portfolio Value	Portfolio Return (%)
Jan-13	11/19/12	690/700 860/870	$2,820	1	no	-$3,220	-14%	$46,780	-6.4%
Feb-13	12/17/12	730/740 910/920	$2,880	1	no	-$2,650	-12%	$44,130	-11.7%
Mar-13	1/17/13	790/800 960/970	$2,940	0	calls	$2,140	12%	$46,270	-7.5%
Apr-13	2/19/13	830/840 990/1000	$2,480	1	no	$2,480	14%	$48,750	-2.5%
May-13	3/20/13	830/840 1010/1020	$2,440	0	calls	$2,240	13%	$50,990	2.0%
Jun-13	4/25/13	830/840 1010/1020	$3,200	1	no	-$1,200	-6%	$49,790	-0.4%
Jul-13	5/20/13	870/880 1080/1090	$2,440	0	calls	$2,340	13%	$52,130	4.3%
Aug-13	6/18/13	870/880 1090/1100	$2,900	0	calls	$2,700	16%	$54,830	9.7%
Sep-13	7/22/13	920/930 1140/1150	$2,260	0	no	$2,260	13%	$57,090	14.2%
Oct-13	8/20/13	900/910 1020/1030	$2,840	0	calls	$2,400	14%	$59,490	19.0%
Nov-13	9/16/13	920/930 1150/1160	$2,540	0	no	$2,540	15%	$62,030	24.1%
Dec-13	10/21/13	970/980 1190/1200	$2,400	0	no	$2,400	14%	$64,430	28.9%

Assumes a beginning balance of $50,000.
Trading commissions were not included.
Each iron condor consists of twenty RUT contracts; at any given time, two positions are open.
Condors were initiated the week following option expiration at about 55-60 days to expiration.
Spreads were positioned with delta of the short option from 7-10.
No profit stop was used.
The long hedge was used when delta of the short option > 18.
If delta of the short option > 30, spreads and the hedge options were closed.
The time stop used the two sigma rule on the Friday before expiration week.

Summary

Trading the iron condor options strategy in a non-directional fashion, month after month, with the objective of steady income generation, is entirely feasible. But a robust system of risk management is essential for long-term success. Establishing the iron condor consistently each month is important, but the ongoing management of the position is crucial to the success of this trading strategy. Beginning condor traders often underestimate the criticality of managing the position. Establishing the iron condor position is relatively easy. Adjusting the position and surviving extreme market events are the skills of the successful iron condor trader.

Two rather different iron condor trading systems were back tested, one where the spreads were opened around thirty days to expiration and the other where trade entry occurred around 55 to 60 days to expiration. The net results for each were positive, but the short-term iron condor outperformed the long-term iron condor. However, the pattern of the returns was quite different. The short-term iron condor system required more frequent adjustments and resulted in larger monthly gains and larger monthly losses. The results for the long-term iron condor system were lower, but more consistent. Traders should always consider not only the potential returns for a trading system, but also the degree of fit or comfort with the system's results when compared with the trader's style and risk profile.

As in our other back testing results, the value of a robust risk management system was proven once again.

CHAPTER FOURTEEN

THE BEST NON-DIRECTIONAL TRADE

At this point, we have established the necessary foundation for understanding and successfully trading non-directionally. The question that my students often ask at this point is: Which trade is the best one for income generation? Much of the marketing in the trading business gives the impression that a particular firm's strategy or trading system is the best trading strategy. Some will even suggest that their system is the "secret system" used by traders on the floor of the exchange. But those claims simply aren't true.

The Myth Of the Best Strategy

In Chapter 2, we learned that the high probability trade with low downside risk does not exist. When our options trading strategy has a high probability of success, it always has a large downside risk. That loss may have a low probability of occurrence, but it will be devastating if it occurs. Conversely, when my downside risk is low, the probability of success is also low. Some sales people will try to tell you that the inexpensive, out of the money bull call spread is a low risk trade simply because the maximum loss is small. But they fail to acknowledge that the probability of making a profit with that trade is also quite small. The extreme example of the low probability trade is the lottery ticket.

The stark reality is this:

All options strategies will lead to a risk adjusted return near zero over the long term.

So the search for the Holy Grail of trading strategies is futile. But that doesn't mean that all trading strategies are equivalent in all circumstances.

Consider the Current Market

How would you characterize the current market environment? Is it boring and slowly moving in one direction or the other? Is it volatile with large moves upward and then large moves downward the next day? Are global events making traders anxious, e.g., wars, riots, governments being overthrown, threats of a nuclear showdown, etc.? The European debt crisis fears of August 2011 and the fiscal cliff fears of December 2012 both resulted in extremely volatile markets.

In extreme market situations, the non-directional trader may be wise to stay on the sidelines and allow the markets to stabilize. However, it is easy to start predicting which months will be good for income generation. In that case, the trader has become a directional trader. The essence of the non-directional trader is resisting the temptation to predict future market direction. But that doesn't mean the non-directional trader ignores the market. I often push one side of my iron condor farther OTM when I am concerned about the market making or continuing a strong move in that direction. When the non-directional trader finds the market environment to be exceptionally volatile, he should take measures to trade more conservatively, e.g., position spreads farther OTM and trigger adjustments earlier.

Where Is Volatility?

Non-directional traders may not be predicting the markets, but they should always be aware of where volatility is relative to its history. The VIX is a good measure of overall stock market volatility since it is derived from the Standard and Poors 500 Index. If you are trading the Russell 2000 Index (RUT), then keep track of RVX.

When volatility is high historically, the non-directional trader may favor negative vega trades such as the iron condor because of the probability of volatility reverting to the mean. When volatility is low, calendars and double calendars will be favored; these are the classic large positive vega trades that will appreciate greatly with increasing volatility. However, when volatility is high, calendars and double calendars have large downside risk. Butterfly spreads have less vega risk; their position vega values tend to be relatively small and negative. Double diagonal spreads have positive vegas, but not quite as large as the calendars and double calendars. As our back testing of the double diagonal demonstrated in Chapter 12, we cannot ignore changes in implied volatility when we are trading the double diagonal.

The iron condor is a negative vega position, but if the spreads are positioned based on a standard deviation calculation, the ultimate profitability of the position is not affected by a change in volatility. When volatility is high, the standard deviation will be large and the spreads will be positioned farther OTM. When volatility is low, the spreads will be automatically positioned closer to the index price. If our adjustments succeed in keeping us in the position until our time stop or expiration, much of the ultimate profitability is still ours. Increasing volatility is problematic for the iron condor when the index moves down enough to trigger the closing of our put spreads, because we will pay a larger debit to close those spreads in a high volatility environment. However, if we hedged with long put options, we will see larger appreciation in those hedge options that will compensate for much of the loss. In my experience, my put hedges have delivered more protection in the downward moves than my call hedges have on the upward moves, simply due to the volatility effects.

How Does The Trade Make Money?

A worthwhile way of comparing the non-directional trades is to consider how each of these trades generates a profit. Calendars and double calendars generate their gains from the disproportionate time decay of the two options. The value of the short option in the front month is deteriorating faster than the long option in the month farther out in time. Another way of stating this to point out the larger value of theta in the closer month, driving larger time decay in the front month. However, vega is much larger in the more distant month and this is the root cause of the large vega risk of the calendar and double calendar spreads. Declining volatility diminishes the value of our long option and destroys the profitability of the trade.

The double diagonal shares at least a portion of this vega risk due to the similar structure with long options in the next month out in time. The majority of the capital investment in the double diagonal results from the higher value of those long options. While the double diagonal's typical position vega may be less than a double calendar, the trader must monitor volatility in the double diagonal just as he would for the double calendar. Declining volatility can easily destroy the double diagonal position. The double diagonal also shares the time decay advantage of the double calendar and gains much of its profit from the higher rate of time decay for the front month options. The double calendar and double diagonal are actually very similar trades.

The butterfly spread essentially is a short option position, where we have sold at least two ATM options and purchased long options on the wings as our hedges to limit the downside risk. The commonly depicted exponential decline in time value during the last thirty days of an option's life is most accentuated for the ATM option, and that is the essence of the butterfly's profit machine (see Figure 4.1 in Chapter 4). Aggressive traders like to sell ATM straddles precisely for this reason. The butterfly is a more conservative, or hedged, form of the short straddle.

The iron condor generates its profits from the time decay of the short options in each spread. Although the iron condor is a negative vega position, volatility changes are not necessarily as detrimental as for the double diagonal or double calendar. An increase in volatility isn't a problem for the iron condor if the trade may be adjusted without necessitating the closing of either spread. The maximum profit at the beginning of the trade is still the maximum profit at expiration as long as the underlying price lies between the spreads. This is true regardless of moves in implied volatility.

Compare and Contrast

Table 14.1 summarizes the characteristics of the non-directional trading strategies we have discussed in this book. These comparative assessments are necessarily subjective; the reader may find his judgment shades these comparisons somewhat differently.

All of the non-directional trades of Table 14.1 are profitable over a broad range of price. Thus, we may allow the price of the underlying stock or index to move quite a bit before adjusting or closing the position. The long-term iron condor will tend toward the widest range of profitability, but we always have trade-offs.

Novice traders often focus on the trading strategies that promise the highest profitability. The butterfly and iron butterfly spreads will generally have higher profit potentials than the other strategies we have discussed. However, two critical characteristics accompany this higher profitability; one is the simple truth we learned in Chapter 2 – higher profitability is accompanied by lower probabilities of success.

Trades with higher potential profitability also display higher volatility of the results, i.e., the range from the largest gain to the largest loss over a long period of time will be larger. It is easiest to see this characteristic by revisiting the back testing of the various butterfly strategies in Chapter 11 and the iron condor strategies in Chapter 13. When we contrasted the short-term iron condor with the long-term iron condor, the first thing we noticed was the superior 73% return for the short-term condor system. But this trading system back test resulted in 5 winners, 6 losers, and one break-even with gains as high as 52% and losses as large as 28%. Contrast that with the long-term condor system with 10 winners and 2 losers, and gains as high as 25% and losses as large as 22%. The range of results, or the volatility of the results, is much larger for the short-term condor trading system. This is typical of trading systems with high potential returns.

Before leaping to the conclusion that the system with the highest return is the best strategy, one needs to objectively assess one's own trading style and risk tolerance. How would I feel about enjoying a 52% gain one month and then taking a 19% loss the following month? Would I be sleeping well if my trading system resulted in six losses and one break-even over the past twelve trades? Or would my comfort level be higher with a string of more consistent winners with smaller gains? The trader can't have it both ways. Systems with large potential gains are characterized by more frequent losses and a wider range of results. But the net long-term gains will be higher. More conservative trading systems tend to have a higher percentage of winners and a more narrow range of results. But the net long-term gains will be lower.

Day traders are often characterized as the extreme risk takers in trading, but the day trader largely avoids one crucial area of risk, viz., what I call event risk. This is the risk of the market making a substantial move at the open tomorrow based on some event, such as war, terrorist attacks, etc., since the markets were last open. The day trader avoids this risk by closing all of his positions before the market closes each day. This can be a significant area of risk for the non-directional trader. The longer my trading position remains open, the more I am exposed to event risk. The long-term iron condor is more subject to event risk than the other non-directional strategies we have discussed simply because we are exposed to the market for a longer period of time. By contrast, the short-term iron condor is least subject to event risk because we are often able to close this trade early for a substantial portion of the potential gains. We may open a short-term iron condor at thirty days to expiration, but have closed the position two weeks later.

Table 14.1
Comparison of the Non-Directional Trades

Comparison of the Non-Directional Trades	Profitability	Vega Risk	Volatility of Results	Management Required	Event Risk
Butterfly	H	L	H	H	M
Calendar	M	H	M	M	M
Double Calendar	M	H	M	M	M
Double Diagonal	M	M	M	L	M
Short Term Iron Condor	H	L	H	H	L
Long Term Iron Condor	L	L	L	L	H

Calendars and double calendars are limited in their use in non-directional trading due to their volatility risk. I use these trades in my accounts on individual stocks and broad market indexes when the conditions are right, i.e., when implied volatility is low. By contrast, I use short and long-term iron condors virtually every month. The varying levels of implied volatility from month to month are self-correcting when one uses a probabilistic approach for positioning the condor spreads.

I have included a column in Table 14.1 titled, Management Required. This column is my subjective assessment of the time required to monitor and manage each of these non-directional strategies. I have ranked the butterfly and short-term iron condor the highest on this measure because these trades can move rapidly, even within one day's trading session. Establishing these trades and then finding yourself in an all day meeting at work could result in an unpleasant surprise at the end of the day. Using contingency orders to close positions when various prices are tripped could ameliorate some of this risk.

At the other extreme, we have the double diagonal and the long-term iron condor. These positions tend to move more slowly because the short options are farther OTM. The double diagonal is even slower moving due to the larger delta of the long options. The long options in the double diagonal effectively provide an internal hedge to market movement. If the trader is unable to watch the market closely during the day, the internal hedging characteristics of the double diagonal spread form a significant advantage.

When comparing the double diagonal spread to the iron condor, one disadvantage of the double diagonal is the margin requirement mandated by many options brokers. For a double diagonal with two $10 spreads, the margin requirement is commonly $2,000, whereas, it would be $1,000 for the iron condor at most brokers. This effectively reduces the returns by 50%. It is principally for this reason that the double diagonal strategy isn't commonly used by non-directional traders.

The Role of Diversification

Stock traders often reposition their investments to ensure the portfolio is not subject to too much risk from either one stock or one industry sector. We call this diversifying the portfolio; it is a method of spreading the risk.

Non-directional options traders should also be cognizant of the value of diversification. First of all, only a portion of one's investment portfolio should be devoted to non-directional trading. I would suggest about 25% or less. Secondly, the non-directional options trader should consider using more than one non-directional strategy in this portion of his portfolio. Consider the comparisons of the previous section above. One distinction in these strategies is exposure to event risk, or the time we are in the position. Thus, mixing short-term iron condors with long-term iron condors would diversify the event risk; a similar approach would be balancing the short-term nature of the ATM butterfly with the long-term iron condor.

If the trader's non-directional portfolio is larger than about $500k, then I would recommend diversification across more than one trading vehicle as well as diversification across strategies, e.g., splitting my long term iron condor trading between SPX and RUT. But the $500k is a judgment call. In my opinion, when we are trading more than 150 to 200 contracts in a particular non-directional strategy, it makes sense to use at least two different indexes.

I am not trying to establish iron clad rules here. I am presenting some of the issues that should be considered in assessing your portfolio risk. In summary, we should aim to diversify our non-directional or income generation portfolio on the basis of:

➢ Strategy – Spread your risk over at least two different non-directional strategies.

➢ Exposure to event risk – Mix short term and long term strategies.

➢ Volatility risk – Consider your vega risk; avoid having high vega risk in more than one strategy being used in the portfolio. One may also mitigate the large positive vega of the calendar spread with the negative vega of the iron condor to better balance vega risk in the portfolio.

➢ The underlying index – Mix it up a bit, e.g., trade SPX and RUT.

Summary

Beginning options traders are often given the impression that a particular strategy or trading system is the best trading strategy. But that simply isn't true. The stark reality is this:

All options strategies will lead to a risk adjusted return near zero over the long term.

This reality underscores two conclusions:

1. Risk management is essential to long-term success.
2. The search for the Holy Grail of trading strategies is futile.

But that doesn't mean that all trading strategies are equivalent in all circumstances. Each non-directional trade we have discussed in this book has its own advantages and disadvantages. And market conditions, such as high or low volatility, may favor one strategy over another at a particular point in time.

There is a wide range of personal style and risk tolerance that determines one's final choice of trading strategies. The butterfly and the iron condor are my first choices for ongoing, month after month, non-directional trading. I use calendars and double calendars on more of an opportunistic basis. But that is my preference. My trading style and my risk tolerance are not necessarily yours.

CHAPTER FIFTEEN

WHERE DOES IT GO WRONG?

At this point, you may be thinking that non-directional trading sounds too good to be true. What can go wrong? Where is the catch? Two different market scenarios present the most significant challenges to the non-directional trader: 1) a strongly trending market during the life of our trade, or 2) a market crash.

Market Crashes

The year 2011 was a good example of the dangers inherent in non-directional trading. Through the first half of the year, most iron condor traders collected nice profits month after month with minimal effort or stress. But the market crash in the first few days of August, and the subsequent volatility in the following months, changed everything. I know of many iron condor traders who lost everything they had gained earlier in the year during August, September and October.

In many ways, August 2011 was an excellent stress test for the non-directional trader. If his risk management system resulted in manageable losses, then it passed the test with flying colors. At the time of that crash, I had two open RUT iron condor positions, one in August and one in September. I closed the August position for a 5% loss and closed the September position for a 13% gain.

Trending Markets

A strong trending market can be just as challenging as the market crash. If you had established an August iron condor on RUT in early July 2009, you would have watched the index drop 7% and then turn around and increase over 20% while you were in that position (Figure 15.1). If you don't know what to do, or even hesitate, that truck will run over you! In this case, I survived that month with a 5% loss after making six different adjustments.

Another example of a strongly trending market occurred in January of 2012, but in this case, the trend was bullish (Figure 15.2). I was trading an iron condor with the February options on the Russell 2000 Index, and achieved a 13% gain after two adjustments. If you can minimize your losses in these extreme market situations, you can achieve profits in the long term trading the iron condor. But that doesn't mean it's easy. It requires a time-tested system of risk management together with sufficient experience and discipline to follow the rules without hesitation.

For iron condor traders employing the long hedge form of adjustment, an upward trending market is more difficult to hedge than a downward trending market because of the natural course of volatility. When markets trade downward, volatility increases; when markets trade upward, volatility decreases. These volatility changes either help or hinder the value of the hedge options. In rising markets, the call hedges do not appreciate nearly as much as do the put hedges in a falling market. Thus, the long hedges are more effective adjustments in falling markets.

Figure 15.1
RUT Price Chart July 2009
Source: *Chart provided courtesy of StockCharts.com © 2014. All rights reserved, etc.*

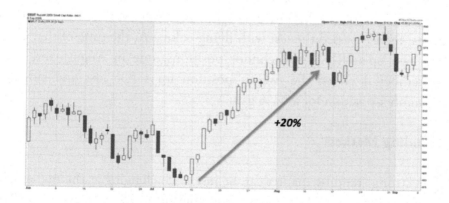

Figure 15.2
RUT Price Chart January 2012
Source: *Chart provided courtesy of StockCharts.com* © *2014. All rights reserved, etc.*

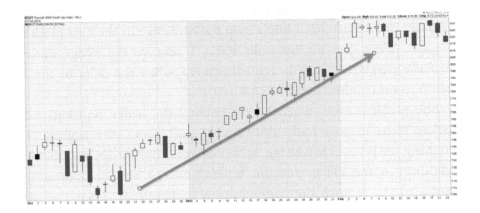

In either of these situations, you must know in advance what will trigger the adjustments and which adjustment technique will be used. I cannot be caught flat-footed and be wondering what to do when the index makes a strong move against my position. Good risk management means I have a clearly defined set of rules (preferably written) and I must have the discipline to follow those rules. Thinking about what I should do after the market crashes is a prescription for disaster.

A common mistake is to revert back to being a directional trader and attempt to predict tomorrow's move while in the midst of the crisis. For example, I might say to myself, "Surely it won't drop again tomorrow; that would be four days in a row. I don't need to adjust here." I think you know what happened the next morning.

My Mistakes

I have traded the iron condor in some form or another every month since 2005. I presume I haven't made all of the mistakes possible, but I have certainly made many of them. Sometimes those mistakes were expensive lessons. So I offer you the benefit of my painful experience at bargain basement prices.

Removing Hedges Too Soon

I use the long hedge form of adjustment when trading the long-term iron condor. Whenever the market trends sufficiently toward one side or the other of my position, I buy a long option hedge in the next month out in time. When the market pulls back, I remove the hedge option. I normally trigger my long hedge adjustment when the delta of the short option in my condor spread hits 18 or 19.

The problem arises when I have entered the hedge position and the market starts to just trade sideways or pull back only slightly. I am watching the price of my hedge option decrease day by day and that loss is weighing on me. That pressure builds and, on several occasions, has caused me to remove the hedge option prematurely. Then the market reverts back to the previous trend the next morning and catches my condor position with no hedge in place.

I now realize that adjustments cost me money – they are insurance premiums. We don't complain at the end of the year when we have to pay our home insurance premium even though our house didn't burn down. The magnitude of the losses on our hedge options is much smaller than the potential losses on our condor position. Therefore, I should err on the side of losing money on my adjustments to avoid a larger loss on the condor position.

I recommend the non-directional trader remove the long hedge when the delta of the short option in the condor spread is two points less than the trigger point that caused you to enter the hedge position. For example, I typically trigger my long hedge when the delta of the short option exceeds 18 and remove the hedge when the delta of the short option pulls back to 16.

Rolling Spreads To Increase Gains

After our long-term iron condor position has been open for two to three weeks, we often find ourselves in the situation where one of the spreads in our condor is far OTM and can be closed for a nice profit. We have three choices:

1. Allow the spread to expire worthless.

2. Close the spread and lock in the gains on that side of the position.
3. Close the spread and open a new spread farther ITM to augment the potential profitability of the position.

All of the choices above are reasonable alternatives. Allowing the spread to expire worthless is a high probability proposition in this situation, but closing the spread to lock in a gain on that side is an even more conservative posture. The third choice of rolling the spread higher or lower is the most risky of the three. The degree of risk is largely a factor of where we position the new spread. The risk is that the market will reverse quickly and whipsaw us out of that position; that can be costly. It is often tempting to position the spread too close to the current price of the index in order to receive a large credit. Resist that temptation. It is perfectly reasonable to collect a smaller credit for the rolled spread in this situation, as compared to the usual credits we may receive when initiating our positions.

If you decide to close and roll the spread on the profitable side of the condor, consider the following rules as an addendum to your trading system:

> If you have fewer than 15 days to expiration, don't roll the spreads.
> Compute one standard deviation for the remaining time until expiration, and position the new spread at, or outside of, that value.
> If the credit for the new spread is less than $0.35, don't roll the spread.

Hedging Too Late

Establishing the delta value that will trigger the adjustment for the long-term iron condor position requires a trade-off. Triggering the adjustment early, e.g., at a delta value of 15, will result in more frequent adjustments over time. And adjustments cost money, so this will lower the long-term returns from the strategy. However, this approach will minimize the losses when the market moves against a position and keeps on moving, forcing the closure of the spreads on that side.

Triggering the adjustment later, e.g., at a delta value of 20, will result in fewer adjustments over time. This will tend to increase the long-term returns by minimizing the "insurance costs". But the price of this approach will be larger losses when the market moves against a position and keeps on moving, forcing the closure of the spreads on that side.

On some occasions, rapid market movement may result in our adjustment trigger being exceeded before we have time to react; that is unavoidable. But using a larger delta trigger value does incur the additional risk of a larger loss due to a late hedge entry in a fast moving market.

I have erred in the past by delaying my hedge entry for a variety of reasons. Sometimes I simply was caught not paying attention. Other times I rationalized why an adjustment wasn't necessary at that time, i.e., I violated the cardinal rule of the non-directional trader: Don't make predictions!

Strictly adhere to the rules of your system; don't delay hedge entry.

Getting Greedy

It is relatively easy to over-trade the long-term iron condor strategy. Generally, this strategy is rather boring. Some of my students have characterized it as "watching paint dry". The temptation is to start actively managing the position by rolling spreads up or down whenever a gain may be achieved.

The long-term iron condor trading strategy can achieve rather large gains of the order of 30% or more each year. That is huge. Those are hedge fund returns. It is certainly true that one could develop a trading system that would be much more active and could probably achieve even higher returns over time. But remember: that only occurs with exposure to higher risk.

On several occasions through the years, I have been burned by failing to take the opportunity to close spreads for ten cents or less. I was focused on squeezing those last few dollars out of the trade, and a sudden market event forced a more costly close. Personally, I have found that I am better served by focusing my attention on the potential return if I close the spreads, rather than the maximum return at expiration.

Our trading system rules are designed to protect us from emotional responses. Our first response to that statement may be to focus on controlling fear, but greed can also get us into trouble.

<u>Allowing Emotions To Overrule The Trading System</u>

The primary purpose of the trading system is to take the trader's emotions out of the process. This is probably never 100% successful in practice, but that is where our discipline comes into the picture. The best example of this mistake comes from my December 2012 iron condor. After the presidential elections in early November, the market started trading down rather strongly. I panicked. When the adjustment for my put spreads had triggered, I chose to close both the call and put spreads and re-position the entire iron condor position rather than following my normal rules for hedging the put spreads. Almost immediately, the market reversed and traded upward nearly as strongly as it had fallen only a few days earlier. I was forced to hedge and then close and roll my call spreads back upward. The position was closed for a loss of approximately two months of gains. If I had followed my trading system, the result would have been a 20% gain.

Follow your rules. Don't allow your emotions to overwhelm your rules.

Summary

Non-directional trading is subject to losses whenever the market trends strongly in either direction or the market crashes suddenly. Following the rules of our trading systems will minimize the losses when these unusual events occur. I have made many mistakes trading non-directionally through the years. The common denominator of these mistakes is failing to follow my trading system rules. Experience in non-directional trading will naturally lead to increased confidence. But confidence may easily lead to pride and tempt the trader to ignore his own rules.

Don't analyze the market. Don't make predictions. Don't panic. Follow your rules.

CHAPTER SIXTEEN

YOU CAN DO THIS

Many different sales techniques exist in every industry. In the options education business, I have observed two related techniques:

"I traded on the floor of the exchange. I know the secret strategy."

This approach is used to sell a particular trading technique. Often the trade is given a special name that makes it appear unique or exotic. A few years ago, one author used this approach to sell a very expensive book hyping the broken wing butterfly spread. He claimed this was the secret trade used by the professional traders on the floors of the exchanges. A pen name was used to increase the mystery.

Another common sales approach uses arrogance and intimidation:

"Look at all of these equations and Greek letters. I am so much smarter than any of you bumpkins."

I have listened to presentations at trading conferences that used complex equations and computer programs to baffle and amaze. But they never clearly explain how their system works – that is a secret. One of my favorite characters uses his time to ridicule all of the common mistakes made by novice traders; he believes his arrogance will serve as an effective sales pitch for his coaching services.

My message to you is simple: You can do this. You don't have to have been a market maker or have traded on the floor of the exchange. That doesn't mean that it is easy or that you will see results overnight.

You can do this.

How Does a Market Maker Make Money?

Many of the books written on options trading come from former options market makers; many of the options trading educators and coaches come from the same background. You have probably seen the pictures of former market makers wearing their trading pit jackets in the advertisements for their services.

Options trading students often assume that the market maker experience is highly relevant and serves as a strong credential for that instructor. So let's examine that assumption. The first step is to clearly understand the market maker's business and what makes him successful.

The market maker for options trading in Google is in business to ensure that you, the retail trader, can enter and fill an order to buy or sell a particular stock option for Google in a timely manner. Many retail traders make the unwarranted assumption that the market maker has taken the other side of the trade and therefore, this constitutes an adversarial relationship. Either the retail trader's prediction is right and he wins or the retail trader's prediction is proven wrong and the market maker wins. But that isn't how the market maker's business works at all. She sells the retail trader the Google call he wants to buy at the ask price. She will continue to make as many trades as possible, buying and selling Google calls and puts; volume is critical in her business. It is a competitive business, but she will attempt to sell options as close as possible to the ask price and buy options as close as possible to the bid price.

In this respect, the market maker is analogous to the used car salesman. He goes to the wholesale auction and buys cars for his lot. He then attempts to sell those cars for as much as possible; we call that price the retail price. To the degree that he is successful in buying at the wholesale price and selling at the retail price, he can make a reasonable profit. Similarly, the market maker in Google options is living off of the bid/ask spread. If she can sell at or near the ask price and buy at or near the bid price, she can make a profit. But that spread may be only a few cents wide. How can she make a living if she is only making a few cents per transaction?

There are two answers to that question. The first is volume; she has to make a lot of trades every day. She cannot afford to insist on only selling at the ask price if other market makers are shaving a few cents off that price. It is a brutally competitive business. That level of competition results in very small profits per transaction. Therefore, a large number of transactions is essential make enough to pay all of the overhead costs from the exchange and leave a profit for the market maker.

We can discern the second success factor for the market maker by asking another question: What happens if Google opens up strongly tomorrow morning and runs up $50? If the market maker happens to be short a large number of calls or long a large number of puts, she is in trouble. Her successful transactions are measured in pennies and this single market move has cost her thousands of dollars. Therefore, the second critical success factor for the market maker is risk management. At any given time, she will know the net delta value of her portfolio of Google options and she will hedge that position with sufficient quantities of either long or short Google stock. In this way, she is indifferent to that large move up or down in Google's price; she is delta neutral. In practice, market makers are rarely perfectly delta neutral; they will hedge their positions to reduce the net position delta to a value that presents what they consider a reasonable level of risk.

Now you can see why the market maker is not simply taking the other side of your trade. She is not your opponent in this game. If everyone suddenly only wants to buy Google call options one day, she will hedge her short call position with long Google stock and then watch disinterestedly as Google trades up or down.

When we understand the role of the market maker and how she makes her living, it debunks all of the conspiracy theories. The market makers are not out to cheat you. The only person to praise or blame for your trading results is you.

Does the Retail Trader Have a Chance?

While it may be a relief to know that the market maker isn't your enemy in the options trading business, we still are left with the question of whether the skills learned on the trading floor are part of the "secret knowledge" necessary for success.

Market makers have certainly learned a lot about implied volatility, seasonal trading patterns, optimal trade orders, and much more. But many of the skills and knowledge necessary to be successful as market makers in the exchanges have little in common with the skills needed to succeed as a retail options trader. In fact, many of the personal characteristics that helped them succeed in those roles may be detrimental to the retail trader.

The market maker must take every trade and he must act quickly; volume is important in that business. But hyperactivity will be dangerous for the retail trader. The successful retail trader takes the time to analyze trade candidates and market conditions and patiently waits for the optimal trade setup. Due to the speed and pace on the trading floor, market makers tend to be hyperactive personalities; calmly allowing a trade to develop over time would be against their nature. Retail traders can afford to be very patient and deliberate and may only trade a few times per month.

Early in my options trading learning curve, I asked a friend, who is a former CBOE market maker, which of the various options trading strategies was his favorite when he was on the trading floor. He surprised me by saying that he didn't have a favorite because market makers don't trade butterflies or any of the other common strategies. That surprised me because the typical former market maker who is lecturing on options trading leaves you with the impression that he traded all of these strategies. He may even offer to tell you which strategy is the "best" strategy. It is true that at any given time, you could separate out virtually any trading strategy from the market maker's portfolio of thousands of options. But he isn't trading butterflies or condors; he is taking as many trades as he can at the best possible prices. Then he hedges his portfolio with long or short stock to minimize his risk. He is living off the bid/ask spread; he isn't trading butterflies.

The non-directional trader has to learn a critical skill from the market maker – risk management. Throughout this book, I have emphasized managing and adjusting the trade. Anyone can teach you how to establish a calendar spread or an iron condor and you can impress your friends at the next dinner party with your strange new language of condors and butterflies. The market maker does not stay in business for long without practicing robust risk management. The same is true of the non-directional retail trader. Risk management is the secret of success for all option traders, including the non-directional trader.

Milking the Cows

When I was in graduate school, one of the other students I met in married student housing at the University of Minnesota was the daughter of a dairy farmer in northern Minnesota. She surprised me by pointing out that her dad never took vacations or even left for a long weekend. He had to milk the cows - <u>every</u> day.

The non-directional trader has to learn the discipline of "milking the cows", i.e., giving this business his complete attention during market hours. The directional or speculative trader may make his prediction about Apple's price move after the upcoming earnings announcement, enter his trade, and take it off the next morning. If his prediction was correct, he profits. If he wants to take the day off and celebrate, he has that freedom.

But the non-directional trader is profiting from time decay in a delta neutral trading strategy. And time decay takes time. It is all too easy to become bored during a sixty-day trade and allow one's attention to lapse. Remember the dairy farmer. Develop the discipline to follow your trading system, including your risk management rules, and maintain your attention. Don't wander off to play golf and be surprised by that afternoon's market sell-off. It will tend to occur when you least expect it.

The non-directional trader also learns about serious business focus from the dairy farmer. Many traders treat their trading as a hobby, not a business. They dabble in it when they have time. The non-directional trader rises early and checks on global markets and the futures for clues about the upcoming trading day. He reviews his positions and notes the "lines in the sand", i.e., the triggers for adjustment or closes. The doomsday purveyors don't fluster him; he follows his rules. On the other hand, he doesn't allow past successes to result in a lapse of attention.

The non-directional trader must never forget his responsibilities:

➢ Maintain your discipline
➢ Follow your rules

- ➤ Manage the risk
- ➤ Milk the cows

Summary

A common misconception is thinking that the market maker has some secret knowledge or skill that gives him an advantage over the retail trader. That isn't true. In fact, some of the characteristics of the market maker that were necessary for success in the exchange, e.g., speed of execution and high trading volume, will lead to a retail trader's demise. Many successful market makers never succeed as retail options traders.

The key advantage of the retail trader is his ability to calmly analyze the trade and only trade when he believes the situation is optimal. The market maker is not the competition for the retail trader; the market maker is not out to cheat the retail trader; the market maker does not make money at the retail trader's expense.

The retail trader must learn the fundamental secret of success of the market maker: risk management. Neither the market maker nor the retail trader will be in business for a long time without robust risk management.

The non-directional trader learns about discipline and focus from the dairy farmer. He treats his non-directional trading as a serious business, and it receives his complete attention during market hours.

I wrote my first book, *No Hype Options Trading*, to pass on my experiences learning the art and science of option trading. I had been disappointed with the marketing hype and option trading myths I encountered along the way and wrote that book hoping to save others from some of those "blind alleys".

This book was intended to help you with the next steps in the learning curve and, in particular, to explain the advantages of trading "non-directionally". I am truly interested in helping you learn to manage your finances yourself and would love to hear from you. Visit my web site at ParkwoodCapitalLLC.com and drop me a note. I personally answer all of my email. While you are there, ask for your free thirty-day trial of any of my services as a token of my thanks for buying this book.

Best wishes for your success in managing your investments. You can do this.

Index